how to start a home-based

Tutoring Business

HOME-BASED BUSINESS SERIES

how to start a home-based
Tutoring Business

Beth A. Lewis

Dedicated to the memory of my devoted mother, Colleen, for her fifteen years of volunteer work at neighborhood schools, but most of all for joyously putting her children first—always. Her love provided me with solid roots and hopeful wings that will last a lifetime.

Library of Congress Cataloging-in-Publication Data is available on file.

ISBN 978-0-7627-5432-8

Printed in the United States of America
10 9 8 7 6 5 4 3 2 1

Contents

Acknowledgments

This book was inspired by my tutoring students and their parents who make my work so fulfilling and fun.

Special thanks to Alexander Kasendorf for his generosity of time and expertise when I needed it most.

Infinite love and gratitude to my husband Daniel, for being my best friend and #1 fan since we were seventeen years old. All I am is because of you and your belief in my every dream.

Introduction

How Home-Based Tutoring Inadvertently Fulfilled My Lifelong Dream

I was born to teach. My earliest and most cherished memories revolve around seven happy years spent at Hearst Elementary School in San Diego, California. For me, school was always about the teachers. When my mother picked me up after my first day of kindergarten, she asked how my day went and I responded, "That Mrs. Boucher is quite a teacher!"

My beloved fifth-grade teacher, Mrs. Taylor, led our classroom with humor, grace, strict fairness, and an obvious passion for her job. She coined nicknames for each individual student and marched us through a challenging curriculum fueled by the power of her full personality.

Sitting at a desk in Mrs. Taylor's classroom, I always imagined myself in her place one day—inspiring students to love an academic subject and overcome obstacles to find success in school. I hoped that someday I could use my personality and curiosity about the world to help students feel competent and reach their academic goals.

My road to becoming a home-based tutor has been circuitous, but I wouldn't have it any other way. After a three-year stint in human resources at a Fortune 500 company, I felt the time was right for me to pursue my dream of becoming a teacher. I didn't want to analyze spreadsheets and push papers anymore. Instead, I wanted the messy challenges and deeper satisfaction of working in my own classroom, teaching third grade in a public school.

Eventually I took a job teaching Honors English and Journalism at a small private high school, a part-time job in the mornings. With my afternoons free, I decided to supplement my income by starting a home-based tutoring business. I lived in the perfect neighborhood for this—a suburban area with lots of school-aged children. After setting up the formal business apparatus, I posted simple flyers on the mailboxes around my home, marketing myself as a full-service tutor who could work with students ages five to eighteen. I wasn't sure exactly how my new life as a business owner and tutor would unfold, but I felt certain that I would thrive as an autonomous one-woman teaching machine!

What I created through my tutoring business is the most fulfilling, productive, and enjoyable professional experience I've ever had. This incarnation of my teaching career has surprised me by the way I feel powerful and valued as an educator.

At first, parents drag their children to me grudgingly, usually after a bad grade on a report card or a series of unpleasant parent-child squabbles over homework. But after a short amount of time, I notice the students coming to organically rely on me of their own volition. They contact me directly to seek out my support and guidance. They arrive at my house ready to learn, trustful of my belief in their abilities, and eager to make progress—even the children who are typically disruptive in the classroom! With my watchful eye and customized expertise, the students come to feel capable of success with what previously seemed to be impossible subject matter.

Since the parents are paying good money to see results from my work, I feel compelled every hour to do my very best with their children. There's no downtime or time to waste. I know that my business depends upon a results-oriented, customized program for each student paired with a respectful dedication to each client.

As a home-based tutor, I am constantly engaged and challenged as an educator because I must tailor my approach to meet the needs of each student who sits down at my table. One hour, I could be teaching second-grade reading; the next hour, I could be working on college application essays. This job forces my mind to remain flexible and active.

I find satisfaction in learning the ins and outs of each student's personality—how they learn best, what unique challenges they face, how they tick. In the classroom with twenty students, I always craved that feeling of knowing each student inside and out; but with so many students to teach, that just wasn't practical. With my home-based tutoring business, I finally feel that I've found the ideal meshing of my personal strengths and professional desires—a fun, flexible way to teach students directly and to empower them to succeed at school.

If you yearn to make a real difference with children (or adults) and are ready to design a unique career in education, a home-based tutoring business could be just the avenue you seek. Perhaps you're a retired teacher who still longs to help students learn. Or, you may be a stay-at-home mom taking a break from the classroom for a few years. You could be a new teacher still looking for that first job in the classroom. Or, you might be an experienced educator who simply craves the flexibility and satisfaction that a home-based tutoring business offers. Moreover, during challenging economic times, home-based tutoring could be an empowering career change at the time when you need it most. I believe that anyone who enjoys teaching, has mastery of a given subject matter, and wants to be in control of his or her own professional destiny will thrive as a private tutor—as long as the business is set up with deliberate care and a positive attitude.

I think of tutoring as the place "where the rubber meets the road" because there's nothing between me and my students—no distractions, no bureaucracy, no superfluous diversions, no hassle. It's just two individuals, working one-on-one to boost confidence and raise grades.

Sitting in Mrs. Taylor's classroom all those years ago, I didn't envision myself teaching students from the comfort of my own kitchen table. Nevertheless, it's been extremely gratifying to watch my home-based tutoring business grow from an asterisk to my teaching career into the true calling I feel I was always meant to fulfill.

01 So You Want to Start a Home-Based Tutoring Business?

By picking up this book, you've taken the first step toward becoming a home-based tutor. Not only are you on the path toward experiencing the professional fulfillment that one-on-one instruction can offer, but you are also exploring the challenges of becoming an independent business owner.

While there are a few formal prerequisites to performing the duties of a tutor, the demands of running your own business are far more numerous and complex (and most likely quite foreign to the average former classroom teacher). That said, with foresight, commitment, and diligence, you will be able to create a home-based tutoring business that will fulfill both your personal and professional objectives.

As with any endeavor, it's crucial to be realistic about what you are about to undertake. With your eyes wide open, you'll be able to accomplish ambitious goals both as a business owner and as a tutor. Throughout the process,

Private Tutoring Statistics

Did you know that according to the *Wall Street Journal* American parents will spend over $4 billion this year on academic tutoring? The private tutoring industry serves millions of students each year and has a predicted annual growth of 12 to 15 percent.

It is approximated that 40 percent of our nation's 53 million children perform below grade level in the crucial subjects of reading and math. Lacking fundamental skills and adequate classroom resources, these children may never be able to catch up to their grade-level peers without extra support.

Famous Tutors in History

- Annie Sullivan tutored Helen Keller with extraordinary results.
- Writer and philosopher Ralph Waldo Emerson tutored students to put himself through Harvard in the 1800s.
- Naturalist writer Henry David Thoreau was befriended by Emerson and eventually tutored Emerson's children.
- Aristotle tutored Alexander the Great in 343 BC.
- Philosopher Lucius Annaeus Seneca served as tutor and primary advisor to Nero, the fifth and final Roman emperor.

feel assured that the personal satisfaction of being a home-based tutor will far outweigh any of the challenges presented on the business side of things.

Classroom Teaching vs. Home-Based Tutoring

If you are coming from the world of classroom teaching, you presumably already possess the subject-matter competence and instructional skills to sit down with a student and teach them something. You've likely been trained at a teacher's college, earned your teaching credential, and honed your skills in the real-world jungle of your own classroom with twenty to thirty students at once. It is assumed that you know how to:

- present material in a logical manner;
- ask the questions that will prompt learning;
- customize instruction to adapt to individual learning needs; and
- assess student progress.

In classroom teaching, even if you teach a single grade level, instructional needs in any given class vary widely. As a result, most teachers develop advanced skills in meeting each student where he or she is at, offering well-planned lessons that suit a broad spectrum of learning styles.

Home-based tutoring requires the intelligent application of all of these skills, but it also demands that you complement your pedagogical prowess with keen

Students and Clients

If you are tutoring adults, your students and clients are almost certainly one and the same. However, with younger students (under age eighteen), their parents are the clients. In this book, the word "students" will be used when referring to the person involved in the learning process during tutoring sessions. The word "clients" will be used in discussions of the more business-oriented aspects of the work, such as marketing and invoices.

business skills that you might not possess yet. You won't have a principal or teaching team to keep you on track or support your efforts. This can be a startling adjustment, at first, and an enduring blessing as you gain experience as a home-based tutor. When you are an independent business owner, you must learn to rely on your own strengths and compensate for your weaknesses through design, trial and error, and hard work.

Running a home-based business isn't rocket science, but it must be done methodically, legally, wisely, and with a positive, disciplined outlook. This book will help you dot all of the business-related i's and cross all of the paperwork t's so that you can get down to the real work of teaching your students what they need to succeed.

Six Things You Might Miss about Classroom Teaching

1. Building camaraderie with other teachers
2. Receiving a set salary and paid benefits
3. Experiencing field trips, assemblies, talent shows, and carnivals with your class
4. Following a predetermined curriculum and receiving the accompanying resources
5. Gaining support from the school team of specialists, administrators, and the parent community
6. Teaching in a whole-group setting

If You've Never Taught Before

Most home-based tutors are trained in teaching theory and experienced at teaching in other settings. But if you lack experience as an instructor, you may still be able to find success as a home-based tutor, with a little industrious creativity.

For instance, if you are a college student looking to earn extra money as a tutor, you certainly have expertise to offer. However, you should be prepared for the lack of explicit teaching experience on your résumé to have potential consequences for your business. How much of an impact will be determined by your own innovation, commitment, and willingness to compromise. One idea is to offer a lower rate to your clients in order to find a place in the market and gain experience as a professional tutor. Or, you may need to offer your tutoring services in more basic subjects, such as elementary math courses. As long as you can attract an initial customer base interested in your services, you will be able to gain valuable experiences (and references) that you can then add to your résumé and build upon for future business development.

Consider perusing the course catalog at local junior colleges (or online institutions) for introductory teacher-training courses. After you've completed a few classes on practical pedagogy, you will be able to add this information to your résumé and marketing materials, thus inviting client confidence in your burgeoning instructional know-how.

You may also be able to learn valuable teaching strategies through reading books. By gaining familiarity with common instructional techniques and educational

Six Things You Will Likely Love about Home-Based Tutoring

1. Setting your own daily and weekly schedule
2. Seeing up close your students' sparks of comprehension
3. Providing laser-focused instruction that benefits your students directly and immediately
4. Watching your students' growing reliance on your abilities and support
5. Earning new client referrals for a job well done
6. Working from the comfort of your own home

Tutoring Certification

There are several tutoring organizations that offer certification programs that may add value to both your expertise and your résumé. Here are some starting points for your research and planning:

The Association for the Tutoring Profession: www.myatp.org

National Tutoring Association: www.ntatutor.com

Tutoring associations specific to your state or region

vocabulary, you will be able to speak more confidently to clients about how you will achieve learning goals. During tutoring sessions, apply the strategies you've learned, tailoring them to complement each student's learning needs. As challenges or questions arise, seek out additional books to move you along in your own understanding of what it takes to teach effectively.

It may also help you to see an experienced teacher in action. Ask a teacher you know or contact a local school to see if you can arrange for a classroom observation. It would be most valuable for you to observe a small-group (rather than whole-class) lesson, as this type of situation will more closely resemble the one-on-one tutoring experience.

To sum up, a lack of teaching experience may or may not inhibit your establishment of a home-based tutoring business. With an industrious, positive attitude and a few concessions, you may still be able to find a niche in your marketplace. No client will argue with quantifiable results, so make that your definition of progress and success, whether you are new to teaching or a veteran educator.

Reflecting on Your Potential for Home-Based Tutoring Success

As you begin to examine the possibilities of a home-based tutoring business, take a moment and reflect upon your current situation, what you hope to accomplish with your business, and how this career change will fit into your life. Like many home-based tutors, you may currently be:

- retired from the classroom;
- taking a temporary break from classroom teaching, perhaps to care for young children;

- looking for your first teaching job;
- a college student with expertise to share;
- looking to supplement your teaching income by tutoring after school hours;
- a classroom teacher looking for increased flexibility and independence; or
- working in a non-teaching field and able to tutor on evenings or weekends.

No matter which of the above descriptions fits your situation, I believe that anyone interested in an adaptable, independent way to make a difference in the lives of students will find great satisfaction and financial freedom through working as a private tutor.

When I first became a tutor, I anticipated that it would be a temporary divergence from the standard classroom teaching path. I was pleasantly surprised by the way that tutoring fulfilled my every professional desire: I could call my own shots, delve deep with a handful of enthusiastic students, and see clear results from my concentrated efforts—all from the comfort of my home!

If this sounds like the kind of business you seek, let's get the entrepreneurial juices flowing by asking yourself the following questions that will help you start to visualize your business and how it will fit into your life:

- Can I offer subject-matter expertise that will be valuable in the marketplace?
- How much time do I have to devote to running a business?
- Do I have the interpersonal skills to work one-on-one with students?
- How committed am I to setting up and maintaining a business?
- Am I comfortable marketing myself?
- How well do I know my community and its educational needs?
- What am I passionate about?
- How can I tailor my business plan to suit my strengths and desires?
- What obstacles (both personal and professional) might I face as I set up and run my business?
- Will I flourish or flounder in an autonomous work environment?

As you answer these questions, you will find yourself gaining perspective on what you want and need from this business, as well as what services you can offer your potential clients. It is not crucial to know exactly how your business will unfold at this time. The most important intangible asset to develop right now is a passionate, positive energy for the business you will create and the students you want to help.

Five Characteristics of Successful Home-Based Tutoring Businesses

- Proven quantifiable results
- Fair hourly rates
- Friendly but firm tutors
- Proactive solutions to assessed problem areas
- Open communication channels between clients and tutors

The Realities of Self-Employment

Classroom teachers have a lot to worry about: discipline plans, scope and sequence of the curriculum, classroom organization, field trips, report cards, and so much more. But they are working within a preset template that has already determined their annual salary, vacations, hours, grade level, health benefits, and basic daily schedule. Their teaching contract represents job security and a known quantity. As a home-based tutoring business owner, you will have the freedom to create your own professional reality, coupled with the responsibility to take care of a variety of important details you likely never considered before.

Owning and operating your own business requires a skill set that is distinct from that of classroom teaching. Thus, it's important to be aware of some of the changes that will be in store for you. As a private tutor working out of the home, you will need to become comfortable with the following tasks:

- Establishing a daily schedule
- Building a positive reputation in the community
- Promoting yourself and your services
- Being self-disciplined and internally motivated to succeed
- Working in a more solitary work environment
- Proactively complying with all applicable business legalities and tax implications
- Meeting your financial responsibilities without a regular, predetermined paycheck

As with any endeavor, there are positives and negatives to the reality of being a home-based tutor. In my experience, the drawbacks feel negligible compared to the plethora of tangible and intangible benefits; in fact, I have become so comfortable with owning a business and being in charge of my professional destiny that I can hardly imagine going back to the world of classroom teaching. With proper planning and execution, I think you will come to feel the same enthusiastic attachment to your business.

Eight Traits of Successful Business Owners

Flexible
Disciplined
Resourceful
Diligent
Confident
Personable
Proactive
Articulate

The Life of a Home-Based Tutor

With so much variety and autonomy, there's no set-in-stone schedule for a home-based tutor. As you set up your business, lifestyle and personal preferences will dictate your typical daily and weekly schedule. If you want or need a three-day weekend, only accept clients for Mondays through Thursdays. If you would like to maximize your income and impact, tutor five or more days per week, from early in the afternoon through late in the evenings. If you are tutoring adults, perhaps you can even tutor in the morning hours.

For example, I tutor part-time and have set aside three afternoons per week for my clients. I created this schedule in order to set aside time to accommodate my writing career and to support my husband's online retail business. So, my mornings are spent working on non-tutoring responsibilities, and I begin devoting time to my tutoring business around 3:00 p.m. on the days that I tutor. About thirty to sixty minutes before my first student, I set up my workspace, make sure I have everything I need for each student, and plan lessons.

I prefer to end my tutoring day at around 7:00 p.m., but sometimes I work later in order to accommodate clients who have scheduling conflicts or special needs. I'm a night owl, so this works well for me. It's up to you where you draw the line. If a student has an important test coming up (such as the SAT), I will certainly consider holding tutoring sessions on weekends, if asked. I know that my flexibility will translate into happy, loyal clients who see results and refer their friends to my business.

Regardless of your business plan and scheduling particulars, there are some common tasks that all home-based tutors will encounter on a regular basis. Here's an overview of the home-based tutoring lifestyle:

Daily

Prepare customized lesson plans for each student.

Procure and set up needed supplies.

Maintain accurate records of sessions, no-shows, and payments received.

If working with clients at home, set aside time for setup and clean-up, and be ready for client arrival at least ten minutes early.

If working with clients outside of home, allow sufficient time for travel and traffic.

Weekly

Proactively communicate goals and progress to clients (and classroom teachers, if applicable).

Tally hours worked.

Update bookkeeping system.

Monthly

Reevaluate student goals and progress.

Send accurate invoices.

Track payments received.

Quarterly and Annually

Pay quarterly and annual taxes according to schedule.

Market for additional clients, as needed.

What (Not) to Expect

If you're hoping to become a home-based tutor primarily to escape the rigors of classroom teaching and to spend most of your day in sweatpants, you'd not only be mistaken, but you'd also be entering this profession for all the wrong reasons. While it's true that tutors do have more free will than classroom teachers, this can be a double-edged sword. As a private tutor, you have no one to rely on but yourself. Your success will depend entirely on the strength of your own personal vision, discipline, and instructional expertise. Clients will sense your intentions, and they always gravitate toward tutors that aim to inspire and uplift their students.

However, if you are organized, optimistic, and talented, you can expect that private tutoring will fulfill the majority of your professional desires. You can approach the marketplace with confidence because you have a quality product to sell—you! Your business will only be limited by how hard you are willing to work. And in my experience, the work itself is extremely satisfying because each hour brings distinct challenges that hold my attention and keep my brain engaged. This career is inherently despair-proof because my fine-tuned actions result in positive changes I can see in both the short and long term through my students' progress.

Eight Traits of Successful Tutors

Creative
Results-oriented
Versatile
Sensitive
Skilled
Curious
Relatable
Friendly

In-Home vs. Mobile Tutors

One of the biggest decisions you will make for your business is where to hold your tutoring sessions. Will you host students in your home? Or will you travel to each student's house? Or some combination of the two? The plans and tips in this book are applicable to both "in-home" and "mobile" tutors.

Enlisting Household Support

If you will be working with your students outside of the home, your business should have minimal impact on other members of your household. Financially, if your family is used to the comfort of a regular paycheck, they may need to adjust their expectations accordingly. On a practical note, you will need to make sure you have enough room in the garage or a spare room to store your tutoring supplies during off-hours and days off.

If you will be holding tutoring sessions in your home, there are more complicated factors to consider. Before you start your tutoring business, begin pondering whether you will be able to procure the following resources:

- *A cooperative, supportive attitude from all members of your household.* In-home tutoring sessions require dedicated time and space that take away from the household's collective resources. The people you live with will likely need to avoid your tutoring workspace during certain days and hours so as to offer you and your students a quiet place to focus and complete your work together. Additionally, all home businesses require support and understanding from extended family, friends, roommates—whatever the case may be. By enlisting the enthusiastic support of the people in your life, you are increasing the chances that your home-based business will be a success.
- *A quiet, dedicated workspace.* Some clients choose to hire a tutor because it provides students with a quiet workplace free from distraction and interruption. If your particular lifestyle or household environment cannot offer this benefit to clients, you may want to consider tutoring outside of your home—for example, at your clients' homes, or maybe a public library. Be realistic about the factors that could obstruct your goal of a silent, distraction-free workspace. These barriers could include anything from noisy or energetic pets and ringing phones to people coming in and out of the room frequently.
- *Organization of space.* Working from your home can become overwhelming and unpleasant if your business tools overflow into your personal space during off-hours. In other words, you and your family will want to feel relaxed at home during personal time without it starting to feel like a de facto office or a classroom. For maximum comfort and efficiency, you will need adequate storage space and organizational discipline to keep your tutoring materials separate from the rest of your personal household space. While a dedicated

home office would be ideal, a home-based tutoring business doesn't necessarily require an entire room in order to function. For example, I use a few built-in cabinets in my family room as storage for my tutoring materials, making sure to clean up my workspace at the end of each day.

So are you ready for the thrills and challenges of being self-employed? Do you have the necessary training, experience, and physical resources to start a home-based tutoring business? Good! Now that you've got an overview of what starting a home-based tutoring business will be like, it's time to move into one of the most important initial steps you will take as you make your dream a reality: envisioning the business.

Self-Test for Home-Based Tutoring Business Aptitude

- Are you comfortable marketing yourself and "tooting your own horn"?
- Do you have subject-matter expertise that will be valuable in your community or target marketplace?
- Are you comfortable communicating with students of your targeted age range, along with their parents (if applicable)?
- Can you be flexible and accommodating of various learning styles and instructional needs?
- How will you and your family adapt financially during times when business is slow?
- How will you assess student progress?
- Do you have the organizational attention to detail needed for owning a business?
- Will you be happy working on your own, outside of a school-site community?
- How will you remain connected to trends and research in the field of education?
- Are you capable of being a proactive, disciplined self-starter?
- Do you have a positive reputation in your community?
- Are you enthusiastically energetic about this endeavor?

02 Envisioning the Business

As an educator with a passion for making a difference in the lives of students, you have uniquely valuable gifts to offer the community through your home-based tutoring business. Similar to classroom teaching, the rewards are not just monetary. You will also discover satisfaction through the gratitude of your clients and being able to contribute your skills to the world. Envision your business bringing joy to the lives of others, as well as financial flexibility to your family. Plan wisely and with clear, positive intentions. Work hard, and then watch your initial vision morph into the reality of your new life as a small business owner. Well-conceived plans will pay dividends with time.

What You Need to Get Started

Unlike opening a traditional brick-and-mortar store, starting a home-based tutoring business requires minimal materials and capital. In fact, your expertise and enthusiasm are your most valuable assets. But just to be precise, let's concretely delineate exactly what you will need to get started:

- Pedagogical expertise and experience
- Subject matter mastery
- A quiet, dedicated workspace to meet with students (either in your home or those of your clients)
- Basic home office (e-mail, bookkeeping, files, phone, etc.)
- A defined target market
- Access to start-up expenses (legal filings, teaching supplies, marketing materials, etc.)

Checklist of Start-up Requirements

_____ Teaching experience

_____ Subject-matter competency

_____ Quiet workspace

_____ Basic home office

_____ Target market

_____ Start-up funds

Defining Your Work Style

One of the perks of creating your own tutoring business is that you can design your work life to suit your personal preferences. You have total control over what the business will look like and how it will function. Here are some of the key aspects you will get to define for your business:

- Where you work
- When you work
- Who you tutor
- What subjects you teach
- What you charge
- When you vacation

As you can see, envisioning your business is a critical step in the process of starting your business because almost every option is wide open to you. The only limitations are your imagination and any demands of the marketplace. Naturally, the more flexible and accommodating you are, the more clients you will likely be able to attract and maintain.

A Word on Flexibility

When you start envisioning your new home-based tutoring business, I recommend prioritizing which factors are most important to you. As a new entry to the market-place, you may initially be required to compromise on some details in order to get your business up and running.

For example, I do not tutor on Fridays or weekends. For a variety of reasons, I prefer to have my Fridays available for outside commitments, occasional travel, and general "breathing room" in my weekly schedule. Over the years, I've only had one or two clients ask me if I could work with their children on Fridays, but I simply tell them that I do not tutor on Fridays and they have readily accepted that.

To compensate, I tutor late into the evenings (I'm a night person) on the other weekdays, so my clients can almost always find another time that works for them on Monday through Thursday. Most families are ready to put academics behind them for the week on Friday afternoons, so I really haven't found my "No Fridays" rule to be a problem. Plus, the practical and psychological benefits of having Fridays off are one of the privileges that come along with the responsibility of running my own business.

As you think about your own scheduling needs and preferences, balance your desires with the impact each decision might have on your ability to accommodate client schedules. Perhaps you will want to finish tutoring each night by 6:00 p.m. in order to eat dinner with your family. Or maybe you have a personal commitment every Wednesday night and thus can't take any clients on Wednesdays. Clarify in your own mind what is not negotiable for your life, but remember that you may need to creatively compromise in order to suit your clients' needs, as well. It never ceases to amaze me how busy my clients are with dance classes, soccer practice, religious school, piano lessons, and so much more. If I wasn't able to be flexible with my own availability, I wouldn't have many clients at all!

Special Requirements for Mobile Tutors

- Reasonable proximity to client base
- Reliable transportation
- Diplomatic communication skills for addressing any distractions in a client's home
- Strong organizational skills

Scheduling is just one of the areas where you will start with a blank page on which to design the business however you like. So let's examine each major aspect one at a time to help you envision the blueprint for your home-based tutoring business.

Where Will You Tutor?

No matter where you hold the actual tutoring sessions with your clients, your business will still be considered home-based because that is where you keep the supplies and process paperwork. Your home will be the central command station, even if you travel to clients' homes to work with students.

Still, as you start to envision your business, one question has the broadest ramifications for your endeavor: Will you tutor in your home, or will you travel to your clients' homes?

For me, this was a no-brainer. I wanted to tutor from my home. I knew it would be possible because I live in a suburban community in one of the nation's top school districts. Moreover, my home is across the street from a school. My immediate neighborhood is teeming with K–12 students whose parents want them to succeed at school.

Yet, in my very first month of tutoring, I was so eager to fill up my schedule and get the ball rolling quickly that I was open to traveling to a client's home. I set up my rate structure so that I offered a lower rate for in-home students and a slightly higher rate for clients that required travel.

I quickly regretted this decision for a variety of reasons. In retrospect, I might even call the ensuing events a "tutoring disaster." First of all, a client misrepresented where the tutoring sessions would take place. (The father called me and said he lived nearby. What he failed to mention was that I would actually be tutoring at the child's mother's house, which was much farther away. It hadn't occurred to me that perhaps the parents didn't live in the same house.) Beyond that misunderstanding, the small rate differential was not nearly enough to compensate me for the time, gas, and hassle of commuting. Furthermore, if I forgot a particular teaching supply at my house, I couldn't tutor as effectively as I would have liked. To top it all off, the client's home was full of distractions, such as loud television sets, people coming in and out of the room, and many pets. I couldn't do my best work, and it was hard to watch my young student's attention wander so easily.

I quickly resolved that I would only accept in-home tutoring clients from that point forward. I believe that there are many benefits to tutoring from your own home, and I communicate this clearly to my clients. If you plan to tutor in your home, I recommend you emphasize these pluses to new clients. Here are the top two benefits of holding sessions in the tutor's house:

- *Control*. You don't need to be a control freak to appreciate the value of setting up an ideal tutoring environment in your own home, maximizing concentration and effectiveness. I can control the noise level, the temperature, the availability of supplies, and every aspect of the workspace. I can ensure that there is adequate desk space, plenty of light, comfortable seating, and no ringing phones!
- *Distance from old habits*. This only applies if you are working with school-aged children. One of the main reasons many parents seek a tutor for their children is because they are tired of the bickering that accompanies the daily homework routine. Their children refuse to do homework in a timely manner and/or efforts at parental assistance turn into full-blown screaming matches. When the children leave their familiar home environments and enter a new space, they can also leave behind poor habits and more easily develop new, positive work patterns. Sometimes, these children just need a little distance, a fresh start, and a neutral adult to help them succeed.

There is a caveat to this glorification of in-home tutoring; as a business owner, you absolutely *must* be realistic about your own home environment. What may be comfortable to you may actually be distracting to your students. If you have family pets roaming around, you may lose out on working with young students who are allergic to or anxious around animals. And while it may be easy for you to tune out your family members grabbing a snack from the fridge, your students will likely lose concentration at the slightest interruption.

If you have even a mildly chaotic home environment, it may be best to travel to your clients' homes for tutoring sessions. You may be fortunate enough to tap into a client base that prefers that setup, anyway. And I can tell you one major benefit to being a traveling tutor: You don't have to keep your house tidy at all times! I do spend a lot of time straightening up my home before tutoring sessions. So, if you will be tutoring on the road, choose to look on the bright side, be organized, and make the most of it. You'll still reap many of the benefits that come along with running a home-based tutoring business.

Special Requirements for In-Home Tutors

- Close proximity to your client base
- Tidy, welcoming home
- Quiet, distraction-free household environment (for hours at a time)

You may even decide to do a mix of in-home and on-the-road tutoring, in order to accommodate your clients' needs. That's the beauty of this type of business. Whatever works best for you and your clients can become your professional reality. Just be sure that you can live with whatever decision you make because it is hard to ask clients to change the routine once it is set up.

Wherever you decide to hold your tutoring sessions, accentuate the positive and make it work for all involved parties. The most important thing is that you create a space where you and your students can learn and make progress together.

When Will You Tutor?

The "when" dilemma is a lot more complex than the "where" question. Even after you've decided on your own daily and weekly availability, you can expect to make adjustments to accommodate the needs of your client base. But before we address those intricacies, let's check out the big-picture issues.

Daily

Ask yourself: On an average day, when can I meet with clients? If you are tutoring adults, perhaps you can work in the morning. But more typically, I imagine you will be working with students who attend school during certain regular daytime hours.

In my community, the earliest a student can get to my house (taking into consideration dismissal times, bus schedules, etc.) is about 3:30 p.m. So as a rule, I consider myself to be "open for business" from 3:00 p.m. to 7:00 p.m. I do prefer to schedule in a fifteen-minute break between clients, which serves as a short restroom or snack break for me, as well as a realistic allowance for untimely drop-offs and pickups.

While I would prefer to be done at 7:00 p.m., I often end up working until 7:15 or 7:30 p.m. On occasion, I have even accepted an 8:00–9:00 p.m. client on a temporary basis, especially if it is a long-term, loyal client. Since I am a night owl, this less-than-ideal arrangement doesn't throw off my whole routine if it only occurs once a week for a short time.

(Keep in mind: You may want to offer later hours for a slightly higher hourly rate. Make it worth your time, and you may find clients who will take you up on the offer. More on setting your rates in chapter 7.)

As you can see, the number of tutoring hours in any given day is limited by a variety of factors. That's why you will need to be flexible with your preferences in order to maximize your profitability and impact.

One of the most challenging times of the year for a private tutor is Back to School time. As clients return from summer vacation with new scheduling restrictions, it can be tough to fit everyone in. Sometimes, the only way to loosen up the schedule is through your own flexibility. Be aware of this going into the situation, and you will feel empowered rather than frustrated or compromised.

Weekly

In almost all situations, the weekly "prime time" for tutoring is Monday through Thursday. On those days, students are school-oriented and need assistance with homework and projects. I recommend being available for tutoring on those days, at a minimum. If your client base requires tutoring on additional days, or you are looking to maximize your tutoring income, add additional days as you see fit. And if you only seek one to two days' worth of tutoring income, set it up that way and find clients to support this business goal.

A Final Word on Setting Up Scheduling

Above all else, make sure that you can commit to your schedule without fail, day after day and week after week. There is no surer way to frustrate clients and sabotage your business than to repeatedly cancel or reschedule with your students. It should be expected that your clients will, at times, need to skip sessions; but as a business owner, you should do everything in your power to minimize the number of scheduling changes initiated from your end. This can be accomplished by defining realistic daily and weekly schedules, and then expressing your professional integrity by keeping your commitments.

Who Will You Tutor?

To teach in a public school in many states, a prospective teacher must earn a credential that specifies qualification for either elementary school or high school instruction. In most cases, making a major switch between one age range and the other requires going back to university and earning a whole new teaching credential.

However, as a home-based tutor, you are immediately qualified to work with students of any age and in any subject matter, just as long as you can prove your qualifications and effectiveness. And if you decide to move up or down a few grade levels, there's nothing to stop you except your own drive to be successful in the marketplace.

When I first became a home-based tutor, I was coming off of several years of teaching third grade, and then a couple of years working with high school students. Embarking on my latest career adventure, I envisioned my new tutoring career as a unique opportunity to combine what I love about teaching primary-grade students with what I find satisfying about high school instruction.

My first group of students ranged from a struggling second-grade reader to a high school freshman requiring help with first-year algebra. I was in heaven! My multiple-subject elementary teaching credential qualified me to work with the youngest students, while I was also able to utilize my rapport with teenagers—all at the same time! And since my loyal students have remained with me over the years, I now find myself helping seniors with college application essays and SAT exam preparation. This diverse age range keeps me on my toes hour by hour, while satisfying my varied pedagogical interests. I love this job!

However, if you're not qualified to tutor first graders in phonics, or if the thought of teaching high school geometry terrifies you, don't be alarmed. Specializing in one particular age range can be quite beneficial to your business, and even your peace of mind. As the community comes to know you as "the fifth-grade math tutor" in your neighborhood, for example, word will spread among your client base year after year. You'll only get better and better at what you do and how you do it, gaining comfort and expertise naturally. And if you ever tire of tutoring the same topic, you can always branch out and try new things with your business. While nothing is permanent with home-based tutoring, it is wise to be strategic and realistic about your plans from the start.

So, it's up to you what grade level you want to tutor and how you want to market yourself (more on marketing in chapter 10). Starting out, make sure that your résumé will be able to support your goals; in other words, you will most easily be able to attract new clients if your training and/or experience speak specifically to the work you want to do with students.

For example, it might be challenging to attract high school–aged students if your teaching credential is for elementary school and you've only taught fourth grade. However, as your reputation develops in the community and you build trust with clients, you may be able to move into new grade levels through the natural development of your relationships.

To sum up: As you envision your tutoring business, play to your evident strengths. Consider what grade levels you most enjoy teaching, because the more comfortable and happy you are with your work, the more effective and successful you will be.

What Subjects Will You Tutor?

Similar to the decision-making process for what age range you will tutor, you will also want to be practical and deliberate with your choices for subject matter. Let's say you have a master's degree in mathematics; it's pretty obvious (at least to me!) that math is your path. Besides, mathematics is one of the most in-demand subjects for private tutoring, so you're good to go!

Also related to the age-range question, if you are determined to work with a particular age range of students, this choice may limit the subjects you can tutor. For instance, you can't tutor algebra if you're working with eight-year-olds, and you probably won't be working on multiplication tables and spelling with a tenth grader.

But beyond these obvious limitations, dig deep and get creative. Play to your passions and expertise. You never know what special skills the marketplace might be craving. If you are bilingual, is there a need for foreign language tutoring in your community? That's a natural fit. Are you a grand master at chess? Consider becoming the neighborhood chess instructor and maybe even starting a club. Are you a musical virtuoso? Music lessons may be your ticket to a fun and profitable at-home teaching business. The sky's the limit—if you can sell it and back up your promise with undeniable results, you can share your enthusiasm and know-how with the neighborhood . . . and have fun doing it at the same time.

A Final Word on Your Work Style

Inevitably, your tutoring business will grow and evolve with time and experience. That's a good thing! Just as I'd never envisioned my teaching career leading me

Questions to Ask Yourself When Defining Your Work Style

What subject(s) am I most qualified to teach?

Which age range(s) am I most comfortable working with?

What daily and/or weekly commitments might interfere with my ability to keep my tutoring commitments?

What special skills do I possess that might be valuable in the marketplace?

If applicable:

Realistically, is my home an ideal place for tutoring sessions?

Can the other members of my household consistently help to facilitate quiet, distraction-free tutoring sessions in the home?

Will my clients feel comfortable dropping off their young students at my house?

back to my very own dining-room table, you may be surprised by the path your tutoring business takes. Start out smart with a focused plan that plays it safe and attracts customers. Then work hard and be open to new ways of doing business. Your interests may move from phonics to physics before this thing is through. You never know . . .

Ways to Meet Your Clients' Needs

Beyond even the wide variety of subjects and ages you can tutor, you will also need to decide what type of tutoring services you will offer. One of the business skills you will want to develop is the ability to be flexible and meet your clients' needs as they arise in new and perhaps unexpected ways. This aptitude will make you even more valuable to your clients and increase the pathways to enhanced earnings and influence.

What Type of Tutor Will You Be?

For now, you're just in the business-envisioning phase. So let's explore some of the key ways that tutors can meet the needs of their clients:

- *Remediation and Acceleration*. Known respectively as "catching up" and "getting ahead," these represent the most common types of one-on-one teaching. More often than not, your clients will approach you in a panic because of a failing test grade, depressing parent-teacher conference, or shockingly bad report card. But sometimes the opposite situation will spur clients to hire a tutor; for example, you could be asked to design a customized accelerated learning program in a particular subject.

How I Found My Niche

When I began envisioning my tutoring business, I knew that I could only attract clients through the specific parts of my résumé that meshed well with the needs of the surrounding community. I was interested in tutoring high school students, but I felt that my résumé better reflected my elementary school experience. Since I had earned tenure as a third-grade teacher in the local school district, I felt confident that I could gain trust from parents of nearby K–6 students right off the bat. Living across the street from an elementary school, I hoped to find a client base very close to home.

Although I had taught at a private high school for a few years, I hadn't formally trained in high school instruction, so I wasn't sure how far I could go in that realm. Nonetheless, I still wanted to grow toward working as a high school math tutor. I knew this was a subject-matter expertise that is always in demand. (Not to mention, I'm one of those nerds that actually enjoys algebra!)

It just so happened that some of my first clients were middle school students. As they aged, I grew with them and accumulated experience instructing high schoolers in a wide variety of subjects, including geometry, Advanced Placement English, and even beginning Spanish. That's how I organically expanded my skill set and résumé to include the subjects I always wished to teach.

As you begin your career in tutoring, focus on your strengths as explicitly demonstrated through the training and experience listed on your résumé. With time and effort, you will be able to find new ways to position yourself in the marketplace.

- *Homeschool Teacher / Independent Study Tutor*. Although homeschoolers are an ever-expanding part of the educational landscape, most parents are not equipped to instruct their children in every subject through the highest levels. That's where you can come in as a subject-matter specialist, ready to complement homeschooling programs designed and administered by parents. This is also a creative way to find tutoring opportunities during daytime hours, not just after the traditional school day ends.
- *Homework Help*. Often, students aren't necessarily behind in coursework, but rather they need a supportive adult for guidance through the daily routine of homework. If homework has become an untenable hassle in the home, parents may seek out a neutral person to help their child complete assignments quickly and accurately. This type of tutoring can also lead naturally into getting the student ready for quizzes and tests.
- *Study Skills and Organization*. Many students are capable of doing their schoolwork well . . . if only they could find that worksheet in their trash can of a backpack. Or, they could ace the upcoming test if only they knew how to make and effectively use flashcards (or other study techniques). That's where your guiding hand can swoop in to tidy up bad habits and show them the wise ways of folders, binders, calendars, and intelligent note-taking. Through your steady counsel, the students will learn how to clean up their acts and be more successful in every area of their lives. This type of tutor is sometimes referred to as an educational coach.
- *Standardized Test Preparation*. There's no denying that there's an obsession with standardized test scores in certain circles. If you are qualified to teach test-preparation skills for the SAT and/or SAT Subject Tests, you could find yourself inundated with clients. You will need to be extremely familiar with the test format and effective test-taking strategies, while keeping up with the latest developments announced by the testing companies. This type of tutoring is high-stakes and results-oriented, so I recommend making this your specialty if you're going to do it. If you are successful, word will spread, making you the recipient of a constant stream of acceptance-letter-hungry high school juniors and seniors. It will initially take some time for you to develop your approach and to design a purposeful course that can adapt to meet each student's needs. But once you've created a program that works, you will become increasingly comfortable with implementing it. Don't for-

get about the TOEFL, GRE, GMAT, LSAT, and all the rest of the standardized tests out there, if that's your cup of tea.

- *Long-Term Project Support.* With this type of tutoring, you can offer students the structure and support they need to accomplish specific long-term goals. For instance, I've recently found myself helping several students with planning, writing, and editing their college application essays. I help them strategize so that they can put their best foot forward in all aspects of their college application, Or, I imagine that someone who is a science geek (no offense) could become the community's "Science Fair Guru," helping students conceive and execute their hypotheses, experiments, and conclusions. It might be challenging to anticipate the long-term project needs of your community when you are just starting out, but keep your eyes and ears open as your clients tell you what they are working on and how they might need assistance.
- *Tutoring Generalist.* I can't imagine many clients hiring an "all-purpose" tutor straight away, but I can tell you that I have naturally grown into this role with some of my most loyal and long-term students. With my very first student, Karina, I was initially hired simply to help her catch up in ninth-grade algebra. But over the course of four years, she came to rely on me for a multitude of educational needs, and I have felt personally invigorated by this relationship. One summer, I helped her complete a summer enrichment assignment that required us to read *East of Eden*, now my favorite novel of all time. During her high school career, I helped her with beginning Spanish, Advanced Placement English, trigonometry, and ultimately college application essays. Now she's attending UCLA, my alma mater! As you build trusting relationships with your students, you can come to play a broad, but crucial, role in their learning lives. As long as you are using your tutoring sessions wisely and showing concrete results, I say, "Why not?"

Realistically, your role as a tutor will likely not fit into just one of these boxes. And that's a good thing! The most effective tutors weave a wealth of wisdom into each tutoring session. So while you may market yourself as primarily one type of tutor or another, it's a good idea to remain open to assisting your students in a multitude of ways. After all, the human mind is complicated and needs a diverse array of tools in order to succeed. If you are a compassionate and curious teacher, you will naturally expand your repertoire in creative ways.

Supplemental Tutoring Services

As your business develops, you will discover innovative ways to help your students reach their full potential. You may want to fold these options into your regular tutoring services for no additional cost, or you may decide to offer them through a separate fee structure. That can be decided at a later time. The important thing now is to be aware of a few inventive ways you can support students in achieving their educational goals.

Online "Consulting"

Providing off-hours online availability to your students can go a long way toward helping them raise their grades and build confidence. One way that I moved my tutoring business online is by offering to review writing assignments before they are submitted to teachers for grading. As you envision ways to take tutoring from the kitchen table to cyberspace, ask yourself, "How can I add value to my services through e-mail or other communication systems?" More on these opportunities in chapter 11.

Coordination with the Classroom Teacher

Coordinating your instruction with the classroom curriculum gives a double boost to your effectiveness by directly improving a student's grade point average and, at the same time, informing you of instructional gaps that need to be filled. Simply ask your clients ahead of time if it is okay for you to contact the classroom teacher. Then procure the name and contact information (I recommend e-mailing the instructors) so that you can introduce yourself and ask for specific ways to complement the classroom teacher's goals for that particular student. In most cases, you will be pleasantly surprised by the symbiotic relationship you can cultivate with classroom teachers, assisting each other for a student's ultimate benefit. In chapter 6, we'll examine this technique in more detail.

03 What You Need in Your Workspace

A home-based tutoring business operates on two fronts—the desk or table where you teach students, and the back-office setup where you manage the business end of the operation. If you are going to be working as a mobile tutor who travels to each client's home, there are other special requirements you will need to arrange in the form of a mobile workstation that facilitates an on-the-go business model. This chapter will walk you through everything you need for all scenarios.

Setting Up Your Home Office

For most people, it will be fairly easy to integrate the bookkeeping and organizational side of the business into whatever personal computer setup you already have going at home. At minimum, the business requires a computer, a filing system, and some storage space. At maximum, you could dedicate an entire room to your tutoring business—perhaps even a downstairs den where you can combine a home office and tutoring workspace all in one easy location. (Wow—that would be nice!) But most home-based tutors will be somewhere in between these two extremes. So let's examine some of the basic tools you will need in order to help the business reach its full potential.

Computer with Internet Connection

Since most people I know are Web-savvy verging on Web-obsessed, I feel confident that you will already have this requirement taken care of. But just to be sure, I'll mention it anyway.

A basic home computer will likely become the communications command center for your business. Busy parents will appreciate being able to get in

Home Office Essentials

Computer with:

- Internet access
- Word-processing software
- Spreadsheet and/or accounting software
- E-mail address

Filing system

Business phone line

touch with you via e-mail on their own schedules. You may also decide to invoice clients via e-mail so that there is a written record of bills, questions, payments, and all client-tutor communications. Your students' classroom teachers will be more likely to inform you of student goals and challenges if they can just drop you a line rather than pick up the phone. You may even want to create a simple Web site to support the marketing of your business. Get online and get creative with the ways that technology can help your business grow and offer value to your clients' lives. It's just good business.

Behind the scenes, use the tools built into your computer to help keep your business organized and functional. By this, I mean that you should create and name new folders to keep business documents distinct from personal ones. It helps to create a folder for each client where you can place all related documents for each individual; this may include invoices, worksheets you design, etc.

Dedicated E-mail Address

I recommend creating a new, dedicated e-mail address for your tutoring business communications. It is free and easy to set up a fresh Web-based e-mail account that will keep your business correspondence from overlapping with personal. For example, I set up an e-mail account with the username "northcountytutor" and use that on all of my flyers and marketing materials. That way, I am not announcing my first and last name, phone number, and core e-mail address all around the neighborhood to various strangers. (I only put my first name on marketing materials; more on marketing your business in chapter 10.) Creating a dedicated e-mail address not only helps with privacy issues, but it also assists you in presenting an organized and professional face to your clients.

Consider creating a customized e-mail signature for all client communications. Include your full name and contact information that will automatically show up at the bottom of any e-mails you send. This is yet another way to show your clients that you take your work seriously as a business owner.

Use your e-mail service's folders function to organize communications by client. (Note: Gmail uses labels instead of folders, but the concept remains the same.) Diligently file e-mails accordingly and you will have handy capsules with all pertinent information for each client, in case of any questions or disputes. It's a good idea to document in writing as much as you can for your business; with so many clients, you shouldn't rely on memory alone. E-mail provides a searchable, permanent record that will certainly come in handy.

Filing System

Classroom teachers often complain of feeling buried by papers and packets. Tutoring won't be nearly as overwhelming, but it's still recommended that you set up a filing system for your business. Some of the folders you might want to create include:

- Individual files for each student by name
- Worksheets and educational materials by grade level and/or subject
- Taxes
- Legal
- Marketing
- Scheduling
- Invoicing
- Financial/Banking
- General Business
- Budgets
- Insurance
- Credentials and Certification

Business Software Essentials

While it's certainly possible to run your business through paper-and-pencil methods, there is much organizational strength to be gained from harnessing the power of software programs. With a few simple programs installed on your computer, you can start your business off on the right foot and maintain a well-run system that will robustly last through the years.

Software Checklist

_____ Word processing

_____ Spreadsheet and/or accounting

_____ Calendar and contacts

Word-Processing and Spreadsheet Software

Most commonly used in the form of Microsoft Word, simple word-processing software comes in handy for making worksheets, designing marketing materials, receiving and editing student essays as e-mail attachments, and countless other applications.

A spreadsheet program like Microsoft Excel offers a multitude of effective ways to organize data, track finances, manage budgets, and control every aspect of your business. You can even use Excel to generate invoices and manage balance sheets. In my experience, spreadsheet software is slightly less intuitive than word-processing software for some computer users, so you might have to play around with spreadsheets a little bit in order to get comfortable with how they work and how they can fit into your business processes. But the rewards are huge, and there are plenty of books and online tutorials to help you along the way.

If you don't already own Microsoft Office, consider exploring alternative software options, such as Google Apps and OpenOffice.org. Both are budget-conscious ways to stock your computer with powerful software that will make your business a whole lot easier to manage.

Google Apps offers a free ad-supported version or a premier edition for approximately $50 per year per user. OpenOffice is a free office software solution that works on all computers with full power and functionality. Both of these options have similar capabilities to the Microsoft Office suite of programs and might be worth checking out if you are open to branching out and exploring new software solutions for your business.

However, if starting your own business is adventurous enough for you, stick with the word-processing software you already know. Either way, use spell-check for quality control and play around with all of the interesting ways you can format documents for the most professional presentation.

Calendar and Contacts Software

Microsoft Outlook is an example of an all-in-one control center for managing contact information, e-mail accounts, and schedules. Alternatively, consider Mozilla Thunderbird, a free e-mail program with optional add-ons for calendar and contacts functionality. By having all of your client contact information and scheduling data in one easy location, you're that much closer to maximum efficiency and organization.

Software Sources

http://Download.com
www.Google.com/apps
http://Office.microsoft.com
www.OpenOffice.org

Accounting Software

The most well-known accounting software is Intuit QuickBooks. Visit http://Download.com and enter the search term "accounting" and explore the free accounting software that pops up. There is a free edition of QuickBooks that offers limited functionality that may still be powerful enough for your business purposes. The full version of QuickBooks Pro will cost you approximately $200.

In my experience, spreadsheet software is easier to use than accounting-specific software, yet still powerful enough for my business needs. I'm already familiar with how spreadsheet software works, and I can combine the functionalities of Word and Excel to generate documents such as invoices. (Hint: Pop the term "mail merge" into your search engine to find tutorials on how to merge data into invoices.) Still, I recommend that you explore accounting software if you are interested; the most important thing is to find a software solution that you are comfortable with and will thus use consistently.

Office Telephone and Fax

There are many ways that a home-based tutoring business owner can set up telephonic communication. Take into consideration your personal preferences and client needs, as well as the following factors.

Business Landline

While a separate, dedicated landline is not required, it may end up being the best solution for your business. If your cell phone doesn't work at your home location or your personal landline is too busy being used by other family members, a business-only landline may be the course you need to take.

However if you want to minimize costs and have other available telephone options, it's all right to skip the step of procuring a separate landline. Above all else, keep in mind that your customers will be happiest if they can get a hold of you easily, while also realizing that you won't want telephones ringing off the hook while you're working with students in your home. Be sure you will remember to turn off ringers when necessary and be vigilant in checking voice-mail messages.

If you decide to use your personal landline for business purposes as well, make sure that your outgoing message sounds professional and assures callers that they have reached the right number. Another issue to consider with this option is that you will have to train other household members on how to answer the phone with decorum, taking accurate messages and passing them along to you promptly. To me, this sounds like a lot of risk factors to take into account, and I would fear a break in the system that could jeopardize my relationships with clients. But if you live alone or can otherwise set up an efficient and virtually foolproof system, go for it!

Quick Tip

Check with your local phone company to see if they offer any special home-business rate packages.

Cell Phone

I use one cell-phone number for both personal and professional communication. With all of my clients' names and contact information programmed into my phone's address book, my caller identification system always tells me who is calling so I can answer and respond appropriately. If an unknown number pops up, I err on the side of caution and answer in a professional tone of voice, prepared to introduce myself to a potential new client. When I am working with clients, I simply put the phone on silent mode and turn the ringer off on my home phone. Voilà—no telephonic interruptions! (While we're on the subject, train your students to put their phones on silent mode, too.)

Voice Mail

If your business phone number doubles for personal usage, record an outgoing message that veers more toward the professional side of the spectrum. Include your full name, business name, and any special instructions to assure clients that they have the right number and you will get back to them as soon as you can.

With any type of business, the surest way to frustrate customers is to take a long time to return their voice-mail messages, or else to not return them at all. Declare a voice-mail policy for your business, such as "I will return all voice mails within twenty-four hours." Then stick to it. Your consistency and dedication to maintaining open communication channels will pay dividends with your clients. You will cultivate their trust and reliance while avoiding a to-do list backlog.

Text Messaging

Most of my clients know that they can always contact me via text message and so they take me up on the offer. It's up to you whether you want to offer text messaging to your clients or not. I find text messaging to be a quick and efficient way to

Watch Out!

If you decide to use your personal cell phone for business purposes, it will turn into not only a business tool, but also a potential pitfall machine. Steer clear of common cell-phone faux pas by:

- always answering the phone in a professional and formal manner;
- letting business calls go to voice mail if you are in loud, rowdy, or otherwise unprofessional surroundings;
- habitually locking the phone's buttons so that you don't accidentally "pocket-call" a client who can then listen in on potentially embarrassing personal moments;
- using formal and grammatically correct language in all text messages; and
- assuming calls from unknown numbers are from clients and answering accordingly

> **Hot Tip**
>
> As you start making purchases for your new business, be careful not to "over-buy" before you know exactly what you will need. You'll save money and avoid waste if you start slow and only buy what you require as the needs arise. Keep all receipts so that you can return any items that end up being superfluous.

verify session times, reschedule as necessary, and even offer encouragement to my teenaged students when I know they have a test coming up. (Example: "Christine—Good luck on your math test today! Remember what we worked on yesterday. You can do it!") Similar to voice-mail situations, make sure to respond in a timely manner to text messages you receive from clients and students; otherwise, you might as well not offer this convenience at all. For students less than eighteen years of age, make sure it's all right with their parents before text-messaging them directly.

Organizational Might = Business Power

The more organized you are in all areas of your business—on your computer, in your home office, and with your student workspace—the more professional you will appear in the community and the fewer problems that will arise. If you are not naturally an organized person, now is the time to develop good habits and stick to them. As the owner, you alone set the tone for the business and determine how far it will go. Organizational snafus will only get in the way of your goals.

Setting Up Your Tutoring Workspace

Whether you will be working as an in-home or mobile tutor, it is crucial to arrange for a comfortable workspace that facilitates concentration and minimizes interruptions. While there may be limitations inherent to any given situation, certain factors are not negotiable:

- Large desk or table that seats two comfortably
- Comfortable chairs (appropriate height for the table, adequate support, ergonomic)
- General-purpose school supplies

- Scratch paper (Bonus "green" points: Use post-consumer paper and then recycle all used sheets.)
- Pens, markers, highlighters, sharp pencils, erasers, etc.
- Ruler, protractor
- Paper clips, stapler, correction fluid
- Textbooks, workbooks, and teachers' manuals (buy used and cheap on eBay or Amazon)
- "Emergency" learning activities or simple games to soak up a few extra minutes before the end of the session, as needed
- Optional: laptop computer with Internet access (can be kept handy to look up student assignments, model online research techniques, etc.)

How To Cut Costs on Textbooks

In the interest of minimizing costs, it's a good idea to get creative when it comes to buying textbooks for your business. Otherwise, you could find yourself spending over $100 on a single textbook that you may only use with one student for one school year. The more you save on reusable instructional materials, the more you improve your bottom line. Besides popping the words "used textbooks" into your preferred search engine, check out the following textbook sources:

- eBay.com
- Amazon.com/textbooks (new and used options)
- Your student's school library (sometimes the librarian allows members of the community to check out textbooks for free, if there are extra copies)
- Used bookstores (particularly those attached to public libraries)
- Thrift stores

Also keep an eye out for teachers' manuals and solutions manuals that will make your job even easier to accomplish with accuracy and efficiency.

Merging Workspace and Personal Space

(For In-Home Tutors Only)

With a constant stream of students rolling through your home, it may take a little extra effort to ensure that your house is work-ready and presentable. Additionally, your workspace should be easy to compartmentalize so that it doesn't infringe upon personal space. With a solid organizational strategy and adequate storage space, your home can still feel like a haven during off-hours, and your students' imminent arrival won't signal a mad scramble to hide dirty dishes.

Transitioning from Home to Work

Once you commit to receiving students in your home, it's important to make the space as pleasant, welcoming, and conducive to studying as possible. Here are some key factors to consider:

- Maintain a comfortable room temperature
- Minimize household distractions
- Turn off all ringers on phones
- Signal "Do not disturb" to other members of the household
- Turn down any music or televisions around the house
- Clean up any excessive visible clutter
- Open windows or spray air freshener to erase any odd scents (cooking, pets)
- Put pets out of the room/area
- Arrange for proper lighting
- Make sure the workspace is brightly lit
- Turn on the porch light to welcome arriving clients
- Turn on lights in any entryways or common areas that students will pass through
- Make your students feel comfortable in your home
- Offer water or encourage students to bring their own bottled water
- Assure students that they can ask to use the bathroom, if necessary

Before each day's sessions begin, it's recommended that you clean up any excessive and visible clutter. A tidy presentation sends a nonverbal message to your students that your home is a place for productivity and professionalism. If they see you blurring the boundaries between relaxation and business, they will assume it's all right for them to cut corners with their work.

Checklist For Preparing for In-Home Sessions

_____ Eliminate all distractions (especially noise, clutter, and odors).

_____ Put any pets out of the tutoring workspace.

_____ Alert other members of the household that a student will be arriving soon.

_____ Ensure that the common areas of the home are tidy and clean.

_____ Stow any questionable items (wine bottles, political magazines, cigarettes—you never know what might raise questions in clients' minds, especially parents of young children).

If any of these tasks will be difficult or impossible for you to accomplish on a regular basis, it would probably be better to work with your students at their homes instead. Be realistic about this at the outset in order to avoid awkward moments or compromised results.

Transitioning from Work to Home

This transition is a lot simpler than the reverse because, after the last client of the day leaves, you will be "at ease" and able to keep your home as you please. It's kind of like after you host a party and the last guest leaves; you take a deep breath, change into sweats, and tidy up the place.

The most important thing is to be disciplined with your clean-up routine. I'll admit that some days I lazily leave my tutoring materials out on the dining-room table for a while at the end of the day. Ultimately, this infringes on my ability to relax completely, making my home feel like an office for longer than is necessary. So more often than not, I force myself to take those few extra minutes to stow all of my tutoring supplies in the set-aside storage space after my last session of the day. We have built-in cabinets in our family room, so cleaning up is rather convenient.

If you don't have dedicated storage space, I'd recommend buying a large plastic storage bin and putting all of your supplies in there. If possible, place the bin in a closet or other out-of-the-way place. And before you know it, the house is quickly spic-and-span and ready for your personal life.

Hot Tip

If you'll be traveling for tutoring sessions, consider buying a filing system on wheels. All of your materials will be in one easy-to-move box with a collapsible handle for easy loading into a car.

Achieving Work-Life Balance

If you're new to working from home, the venture may present special challenges as you figure out how to merge an active household with a growing business. As much as possible, try to create systems and routines that keep your personal resources and business tools functionally separated, yet still conveniently accessible to both sides of your new life.

Besides separating out your business files from the personal (in both paper and electronic forms) and stowing your tutoring tools when you're off-duty, it's a good idea to mark a delineation between what you need to get done as a business owner and what you must accomplish as a private individual. One easy way to do this is through creating two separate (and ongoing) to-do lists. That way, you can check off tutoring-related tasks during your office hours. Then you can switch gears to

Sample Daily To-Do LIst

Daily Personal Tasks	Daily Business Tasks
1.	1.
2.	2.
3.	3.
4.	4.
5.	5.
6.	6.
7.	7.
8.	8.
9.	9.
10.	10.

personal activities when you've closed up shop for the day. Try to list the tasks in order of priority, if possible, so that the most time-sensitive items are completed first. Check off tasks as they are finished, adding new activities as they arise.

Creating a Mobile Workspace

(For Traveling Tutors Only)

On-the-go tutors will need to devise an additional level of organization for their business because they must carry with them everything necessary to be effective teachers. Nothing brings learning to a screeching halt like forgetting a necessary workbook, foreign language dictionary, or even something as basic as a ruler or calculator. Ideally, your students will be able to pick up the slack and provide the missing supply from their personal stashes, but you shouldn't count on it.

Clients are paying you to show up at their homes ready to make learning magic happen. By designing a well-planned mobile workstation, you can get in, get going, and get out smoothly and quickly. I recommend using a filing system on wheels, with perhaps an additional plastic storage box on top for non-paper essentials such

Questions to Ask When Preparing for Mobile Sessions

Do I have the textbooks I need?

Do I have the school supplies I need?

Will I need a calculator, ruler, protractor, or other tool?

Have I placed the materials for my next student in a handy spot?

Do I have sharpened pencils, if needed?

Do I have adequate directions to where I'm going?

Have I allowed enough time for traffic, parking, and getting settled in the client's home?

Do I have my recordkeeping materials?

Have I left enough time to get to my next client?

Did I bring extra learning activities in case of a little extra time or unforeseen complications?

as writing utensils and learning tools. Arrange it so that the materials you need for the student at hand are on top and easy to access; don't waste your client's time and money digging through supplies to find what you need.

At the beginning of your home-based tutoring career, you may forget a few key instructional ingredients; just get creative and make the best of it, and learn from your mistakes so it doesn't happen again. After all, as teachers, we aim to be role models for our students. Mobile tutors will have to work extra hard to present an organized and ready-to-go front even while on the go and all around town.

Use the above list for "Setting Up Your Tutoring Workspace" as a starting point, and tack on additional materials as you find them necessary. Mobile tutoring may require a little more forethought and planning, so you may consider charging slightly higher rates for this type of work. Consider giving your clients the option. This issue will be addressed further in chapter 7, but start mulling it over now to see how it might work best for you.

A Final Word on Workspaces

What you need in your tutoring business workspace will vary greatly, and will depend upon individual circumstances, subjects and grade levels taught, your particular client base, and your teaching style. It should go without saying that if you will be offering piano lessons, you will need a piano in your home or at your clients' residences. The key lesson from this chapter should be that it's critical to contemplate how you can create the most comfortable and efficient tutoring atmosphere for your students. Outside of the four walls of a traditional classroom, the home must become a serious learning environment. This won't happen without the business owner's clear intentions and serious legwork. Be prepared, be a leader, and always strive to improve upon the procedures you've established. Organization and diligence will be your greatest assets in this endeavor.

04 Writing a Business Plan

As you begin the hard work of making your entrepreneurial dreams a reality, a thoughtfully written business plan will serve as your blueprint. A business plan clarifies your intentions, communicates your objectives to professionals whose help you seek, and keeps you on track toward meeting both short- and long-term goals. With strategic planning and an ambitious vision, your business plan will reflect your strengths, your hopes, and the financial realities of your new life as a business owner.

Why Create a Business Plan?

You should write a business plan for three reasons, at the very least:

1. To determine whether a home-based tutoring business will be able to meet your financial needs
2. To increase your chances of success by taking the time to examine how your strengths fit into the marketplace
3. To establish and communicate short- and long-term plans for your business

After you write your business plan, you may discover additional benefits from the process. Most likely, you will notice a few fresh strategies that came to mind as you went through the process of formally writing down your plans. But for now, it's enough to know that writing a business plan is an essential and doable step in the entrepreneurial process.

Elements of the Business Plan

There are as many distinct ways to write a business plan as there are business ideas in the world. Don't get overwhelmed by a myriad of examples or the

Hot Tip

As you write your business plan, imagine you're writing it for an audience of investors. For enterprises that require major outside funding, business plans can facilitate earning a "green light" for owners' dreams. However, with a home-based tutoring business, financing is likely not a serious concern because start-up costs are so low. Still, as you write the business plan, you will strike the right tone if you imagine you are trying to convince investors to come on board and buy a stake in your endeavor.

"right" vs. "wrong" way of writing a plan; they can vary greatly in length and format based on the nature of the business.

To streamline your efforts and get you started, I've explored a variety of business plan formats, picking and choosing the sections that complement the particular needs of a home-based tutoring business owner.

The six recommended sections of your business plan are:

- Description of Business
- Business Vision and Objectives
- Mission Statement and Educational Philosophy
- Marketing Plan
- Operating Plan and Policies
- Projected Monthly Costs vs. Income

Of course, you may customize this business plan template to meet your own situation and preferences, but I suggest that you begin with this core framework to ensure that you've covered the fundamentals.

Business plans are detailed documents that outline what you hope to accomplish with your business and how you plan to do it. Even if this is your first foray into entrepreneurialism, don't be intimidated by the task of writing a business plan. On the other hand, don't be fooled into thinking this is a superfluous step in your new career's development. Writing a business plan isn't rocket science, but it does represent a critical step in the path toward defining and, thus, achieving your business goals.

Benefits of a Business Plan

The process of writing a business plan gives you:

- Personal clarity
- Entrepreneurial focus
- Specific goals (both short- and long-term)
- A realistic financial snapshot

You'll find a complete sample business plan later in this chapter. But first, let's explore the core components of the home-based tutoring business plan.

Description of Business

This is the most important section of the business plan because it serves as an introduction to the structure of your business. Here, you will write a straightforward synopsis of your endeavor's big picture. Some of the aspects you may wish to include are:

- Who you will tutor
- How you will tutor (at home, mobile, a mix)
- What subjects you will tutor
- A key point or two from each of the sections that follow
- Data that shows why your business will find a viable market

End with a statement of the purpose of the business plan itself, informing the audience of what insight they should expect to gain from reading the plan. The overall tone of this section should balance enthusiasm with realism while inspiring the reader to explore the rest of the business plan.

Business Vision and Objectives

The Vision for your business can be one to three succinct sentences that express the idealized outcome you foresee creating through your work. Your Vision should be clear, concise, and memorable, providing specific, detailed focus for your efforts.

Objectives are similar to Vision, but longer and more detailed. This is the place to delineate your short-, medium-, and long-term goals for the business. These goals can include your objectives for your students as a group, as well as for the business as its own financial entity. As you write your Objectives, imagine you are telling a short story about how your business will add value to the community, meet the needs of clients, develop with time, and fulfill its ultimate goals.

Mission Statement and Educational Philosophy

In my view, setting forth one's intentions for the company is fundamental to achieving goals and making a difference in the community. Prospective home-based tutoring business owners who seek only financial gain or an "easy" schedule will find their business stifled by greed and shortcuts, whether or not the individual is aware of it or not.

Clients can sense your motives, so take this time to get in touch with why you really want to tutor, what you hope to accomplish, and what you believe about teaching as a professional endeavor. An educator who purely aims to help students meet learning and life goals is creating a business that will emanate positivity and a "can-do" attitude. This attracts students who will truly appreciate and benefit from your expertise.

To complement your Mission Statement, this section offers the opportunity to express your Educational Philosophy. This is a paragraph or two that sums up what your personal beliefs about student potential, the learning process, the instructional process, and much more. You may have already written your Educational Philosophy in a teaching credential program while studying to enter the field of education. If so, update your thoughts, expanding on the core sentiments to fit your new instructional model as a home-based tutor. It's a good idea to review your Educational Philosophy once or twice a year, in order to ensure that you are on task and in alignment with your core beliefs about a teacher's role in the learning process.

Marketing Plan

This section is your opportunity to state how your customers will benefit from your services and why your skills are needed in the marketplace. Delineate the unique services you will offer clients, how you will attract new business, and how your company will meet the needs of your community. Some of the key questions to answer here include:

- What is your pricing strategy?
- How specifically will you market your business?
- What special skill set do you bring to the position of tutor?
- How will you compete with other tutoring services in the area (including corporate tutoring centers, other private tutors, etc.)?
- How will you use the Internet to market your business?

You may need to perform some market research in order to get a realistic sense of your community's needs and how you will fit into the marketplace. This could be as simple as casually surveying a handful of parents at the local school—or perhaps you could offer a free hour of tutoring services to parents who help you complete a fact-finding survey. Get creative, get information, and use this time writing your business plan as a chance to examine all aspects of what will make your business successful.

It is recommended that you read through the later sections in this book about marketing and setting prices before completing this section of the business plan. The marketing strategies for a home-based tutoring business differ greatly from those for a retail business with physical products to sell, so you will want to gather as much industry-specific information as you can before setting your strategy.

Operating Plan and Policies

In this part of the business plan, you will outline how the business will function on a day-to-day basis. Explicitly plan your proposed daily and weekly schedule, the location of tutoring sessions, invoicing and payment processes, and operating expenses. Also consider how you will assess and communicate student progress. On the policy side, lay out your guidelines for late payments, cancellations, no-shows, and other structures you need to have in place to maintain an orderly and fair relationship with clients.

Projected Monthly Costs vs. Income

For brick-and-mortar businesses with rents to pay and product shelves to stock, this is where it gets complicated. For home-based tutoring entrepreneurs, this is where you will breathe a sigh of relief and feel gratitude for a relatively simple business model.

Start-up and ongoing costs are low, but it's still important to create a spreadsheet blueprint for how your business finances might look in the first six months to one year of business. Do your best to estimate how many clients you will be able to attract and maintain throughout a given year. I recommend appraising costs on the high end and income on the low end just to be cautious. As you work through this section, you'll start to see a clearer picture of your financial prospects as a new business owner. See chapter 7 for more detailed information on budgets.

How Will You Define Business Success?

As a separate entity from the official business plan, let's examine how you define success for your business. Beyond your intentions and mission statement, how exactly will you know that your business is a "success"?

How I Define Success

Rather than emphasizing financial metrics, I have built my business on the premise that my expertise and attitude will attract the clients and resources that my business needs to grow. So I primarily focus on other measurable ways to know that I am fulfilling my potential as a tutor and as a business owner. My criteria for success are:

Improved student performance: Results must be concretely assessed by standardized test scores, grade point averages, test/quiz results, or other measurable educational goals.

Client retention rate: If my clients choose to stay with me year after year, I can assume they are pleased with the results and the experience.

The fullness of my schedule: I will know that I am marketing my business effectively if I am booked for 80 to 100 percent of my available tutoring hours.

Essentially, I direct my energies toward goals that develop my professional pride and career satisfaction; in turn, these very factors lead to proven results and a positive attitude, ultimately building my reputation in the community.

The definition of a business's success is a very personal issue. In my own experience, I would estimate that my reasons for becoming a home-based tutor were 50 percent to find personal/career satisfaction and 50 percent to contribute to the household finances. Now that I have been in business for several years, I find that I love my job and the financial freedom it brings. So I would consider my business an over-the-top, beyond-my-wildest-dreams success. I've helped many struggling young students raise their grades, feel more confident, and reach their short- and long-term goals. I control my own rates, set my own schedule, and manage my professional growth—all from the comfort of my own home. From my perspective, I couldn't ask for a more successful business. Going forward, I hope I can continue to grow my client base and find new challenges for myself professionally.

Your motivations may be a different mix of the abovementioned factors, or a potpourri of a few additional reasons. These goals for your business will help determine how you measure its success over time. So take a few moments to envision yourself and your business in approximately one to two years. What circumstance or outcome will make you grateful and proud of your decision to become a home-based tutor? When setting your metrics for success, be concrete in the financial arena and idealistic in regard to your personal growth. Write it down for clarity and refer back to it often to help with goal-setting and to make sure your business is on the right track.

Summing Up the Business Plan

Congratulations! You've finished writing your business plan. You have designed a formal document that represents the intentions, dreams, and practicalities surrounding your new "baby." Now that you've done all this work, don't just let your business plan languish in a dusty file cabinet. Refer back to it every so often as a sort of touchstone that refreshes your vision and commitment.

At this stage in the business-starting game, enthusiasm is usually high, ambitions are revving up, and you're ready to take the first tangible steps toward setting up your legal business apparatus. Take a deep breath and prepare to make it official!

DESCRIPTION OF BUSINESS

Jane Smith Tutoring Services is a sole proprietorship serving the Brentwood community of Los Angeles, California. As the business's owner and sole tutor, I have experience teaching kindergarten through sixth-grade students. Subject areas of expertise include elementary mathematics, reading, and writing. Tutoring sessions will be held in my home in Brentwood. The target market will be K–6 students who need to remediate or accelerate learning in the subjects of math, language arts, or general study skills.

Jane Smith Tutoring Services expects to find success in the private tutoring industry because it is estimated that up to 40 percent of our nation's students are performing below grade level. These students will need supplemental instructional support in order to catch up to grade-level performance standards. Parents spend approximately $4 billion nationwide each year on academic tutoring. The private tutoring industry serves millions of students per year and has a predicted growth of 12 to 15 percent per year. In the Brentwood area alone, there are approximately three elementary schools, translating to nearly 2,000 K–6 students.

As the sole proprietor of Jane Smith Tutoring Services, I bring my ten years of classroom teaching experience to the business, as well as my expertise in test preparation. I am trained in the latest instructional strategies for elementary-school-aged students.

The following Business Plan will delineate the key goals, philosophies, policies, and financial data that will contribute to the overall success of the business. I look forward to combining my ambitious vision with these practical plans as I build a solid business foundation.

BUSINESS VISION AND OBJECTIVES

As the owner and operator of Jane Smith Tutoring Services, I aim to create a profitable tutoring business that meets the needs of my surrounding community by providing friendly, affordable, and top-quality tutoring services. I envision providing my clients with maximum educational value through my highly customized instructional expertise, assessing and then meeting each individual's learning goals. I want to build lasting relationships with my students and clients based on mutual respect and communication.

One of the business's short-term objectives is to tap into a local client base that needs private K–6 tutoring. My goal is to immediately begin building a positive reputation in the community as a competent and friendly instructor. With time, word-of-mouth will become a primary marketing tool as my business's reputation leads to an increased numbers of new client referrals. A primary long-term business objective is to find creative ways to expand the tutoring services into the online arena. I also plan to develop new skill sets and grow with my students, so that I can take on clients of older age ranges and new academic subjects.

MISSION STATEMENT AND EDUCATIONAL PHILOSOPHY

The mission for Jane Smith Tutoring Services is to serve as an educational leader in the community through one-on-one tutoring sessions. I am starting this business in order to match my particular strengths as an expert in elementary math and language arts instruction with students who can benefit from the knowledge I have to offer. I want to help children and families who feel lost or frustrated with a particular learning task to discover the feeling of success that comes with customized instructional guidance.

- The following represents my personal educational philosophy:

  I believe that a teacher is morally obligated to hold only the highest of expectations for each and every one of her students. Thus, the teacher maximizes the positive benefits that naturally come along with any self-fulfilling prophecy; with dedication, perseverance, and hard work, her students will rise to the occasion.

- I aim to bring an open mind, a positive attitude, and high expectations to every tutoring session. I believe that I owe it to my students, as well as the community, to bring consistency, diligence, and warmth to my job in the hope that I can ultimately inspire and encourage such traits in the children as well.

MARKETING PLAN

The target market is the parents of the nearly 2,000 elementary school students in the surrounding area. Some of these parents may seek remediation to help get their children performing at grade-level standards, while others may ambitiously pursue accelerated instruction that offers customized challenges for their children. Due to the range of tutoring services offered, a large percentage of K–6 students in the community may be interested in hiring a private tutor to meet their educational goals.

Our competition will consist mainly of corporate tutoring centers. Jane Smith Tutoring Services can offer advantages over the competition because of our casual, personal approach that makes students comfortable, as well as our low overhead that results in competitive hourly rates. Additionally, all instruction is delivered by one known-quantity tutor that each student can develop a relationship with over time.

The marketing plan consists of posting flyers in the community, attracting users to the business's Web site through Google AdWords, contacting parents of former students, utilizing free advertising on Craigslist, and eventually word of mouth and client referrals. I will offer loyal customers the opportunity to lock in their low hourly rates for a set period of time, in exchange for continuous patronage. Through the business Web site at JaneSmithTutoring.com, prospective clients will be able to view my résumé, testimonials from satisfied clients, answers to frequently asked questions, and contact information for further inquiry.

OPERATING PLAN AND POLICIES

All tutoring sessions will take place in my home between the hours of approximately 3:00 p.m. to 7:00 p.m., Monday through Thursday. Clients will be invoiced on a monthly basis, on the first of each month for the prior month's activity. Payments are due within ten days. Late payments are subject to a $10 late fee. A scheduled tutoring session may be canceled at least twenty-four hours in advance without penalty. Cancellations within twenty-four hours are subject to the following penalties:

- $10 for the first late cancellation
- 50 percent of the hourly rate for the second late cancellation
- 100 percent of the hourly rate for the third late cancellation
- "No shows" without a phone call will be required to pay 100 percent of the hourly rate.
- All reasonable extenuating circumstances will be taken into account. Repetitive late cancellations and/or "no shows" may result in termination of tutoring services.

Operating expenses will be minimal and will consist mainly of basic school supplies, such as paper and writing utensils. Larger-ticket items may include textbooks and other instructional tools as needs arise.

PROJECTED MONTHLY COSTS VS. INCOME

Initial start-up costs are estimated to be $400–$700. As detailed in the Projected Monthly Budget, ongoing monthly costs are projected to be approximately $75, with a projected total monthly income of $1,000.

05 Getting Started

This is the moment you've been waiting for! It's time to strap on your seat belt, get into the driver's seat, and make real progress toward tutoring your very first student. You've envisioned your new career, set up your home office, written the business plan, and defined your goals. Now it's time to install the formal apparatus for your business. With research, diligence, and attention to detail, your business will be officially started very soon.

You should feel empowered and energized by the progress you've already made, so don't let the following bureaucratic steps in the process intimidate or discourage you. If you come from the world of classroom teachers, it's likely you never imagined yourself filing for a business license or worrying about tax implications. That's okay; it's not nearly as complicated as it may sound. And if any concerns or complications arise, you can always consult qualified professionals to help you comply with local laws and make the most of your new income stream.

Setting Up Your Small Business

While there are some basic business-starting steps common to all parts of the United States, it's important to realize that each city, county, and state has its own set of statutes and restrictions when it comes to opening and operating a small business. Hence, you'll want to reach out to experts in your surrounding community for guidance and support. These local experts may include representatives from regional small business groups or professionals you hire to guide you along the path toward officially setting up your business.

Pay special attention to detail during this time so that your business is set up correctly from the start. That way, you can avoid having to go back and revisit the process at a later date. Having to ultimately undo any errors or

A Word about Online Research

The Internet is a powerful research tool for virtually any topic, including how to start a business. However, the wise researcher knows that just because a piece of information is online doesn't mean it is fact. Confirm all important information with phone calls to local and state government offices. Verify results by cross-referencing a variety of sources. Talk to other small business owners to see what worked for them. It's a good idea to be skeptical and diligent when using the Internet to learn about any topic, but especially when it involves the high-stakes venture of starting your own business.

inefficiencies will cost you precious time and business resources. But with proactive planning and research, setting up your home-based tutoring business should be a relatively painless process.

Do Your Research

It's a cliché, but true: Information is power. If you've never started a business before, it's important to do your research about what is required legally. By familiarizing yourself with the business basics for your state, you are gaining a valuable knowledge base that will serve you well throughout your tenure as a business owner. As you do research, take notes on specific questions that you may later take to professionals, such as a business attorney or accountant.

Your local Small Business Association (SBA) is a strong starting point for your research. This federal agency helps Americans start, build, and grow businesses through a network of field offices, so you'll want to find the one nearest you. The SBA Web site can help you set up a health savings account, learn about local laws and regulations, and apply marketing strategies to grow your business.

Steps to Starting Your Business

Although it's always wise to verify state and local business regulations, there are a few basic steps that will need to be considered by all home-based tutoring business owners.

Helpful Sites to Support and Inform Small Business Owners

Entrepreneur.com: www.entrepreneur.com/bizstartups
Internal Revenue Service: www.irs.gov
LegalZoom: www.legalzoom.com
Service Corps of Retired Executives (SCORE): www.score.org
Small Business Association (SBA): www.sba.gov

File for a Business Name and/or License

In almost all cases, an individual starting a home-based tutoring business will want to form a sole proprietorship. This business structure is an easy and inexpensive way to set up your tutoring business. Essentially, a sole proprietorship legally defines you and your business as a single entity. This means that you are solely responsible for any and all liabilities that may arise during the course of doing business.

If you are going to be doing business under a chosen company name (for example, "Hi-Score Tutoring Services"), then you need to file for a DBA which stands for "doing business as." Also known as a Fictitious Business Name (FBN), it serves to inform the public that you are the sole proprietor of a business operating under a stated name.

You may also opt to run your business as a consultant or individual contractor (i.e., in your own name rather than under a business name). In that case, you do

A Word about Naming Your Business

If you choose to file a DBA/FBN, choose a business name that reflects your discipline, goals, or philosophy. Select a positive, easy-to-remember name that reflects the distinct aspects of your business. For example:

Ace Math Tutor
SAT Star Tutoring
Hi-Score Tutor
Reading Adventures Tutoring

not need to file for a DBA or FBN. You would simply need to file for a local business license. Consult your state's online business portal for detailed information on what exactly is required and how to file for a business license.

If your business eventually develops more complex needs or goals, you can always change the structure of your business at that time; other options include a general partnership or Limited Liability Company (LLC). But a sole proprietorship is an easy and practical way to start your tutoring business for now.

Open a Business Bank Account

Most banks require a DBA and/or business license in order to open a business banking account. So once the appropriate paperwork has gone through, take the documents to the bank. Arrange for a new business account through which you can run all of your business income and expenses. All incoming cash and checks should be deposited into your business bank account. You may even want to open a dedicated credit card to use for all business purchases. One of the benefits to this is that your

Filing Legal Documents Without an Attorney

What should you do if you are hesitant to handle the bureaucracy of starting a business on your own, but you don't want to pay costly legal fees with a business attorney?

One affordable way to file dependable legal documents is to skip the high costs of hiring an attorney and instead use an online legal documents service. The most well-known of such sites is www.LegalZoom.com, but there are many other such services out there.

For a modest fee, a do-it-yourself legal site walks you through the steps of starting a business and even files the appropriate paperwork for you. Using LegalZoom (or similar) is a fine compromise between doing it yourself and paying the high hourly rates that business attorneys charge. The service will take into account what state you are in and present all of your options in easy-to-compare charts. You can use this site to file for a DBA and set up a sole proprietorship, or even to compose documents you hopefully will never need, such as a late payment collection letter for overdue clients.

monthly credit card statement will provide an at-a-glance statement of all business-related charges. In combination with saving all of your receipts, this will make for easy accounting come tax time.

Some banks may even be able to help you secure health insurance and set up Health Savings Accounts. As your business grows with time, you will perhaps need to rely on the team at your local bank for additional resources, such as payroll services. Get to know your banker and look for ways to maximize the power and efficiency of your business through their small business services.

Procure Insurance

As a sole proprietor of your business, you are personally responsible for any liabilities that the business incurs. Thus, it's better to be safe than sorry when it comes to insuring your business.

If you will be traveling to your clients' homes for tutoring sessions, you will likely be covered by their homeowners' insurance policies for guests entering the home. Check with an insurance professional to verify. This may be the one area where traveling tutors have a simpler path than at-home tutors.

In contrast, if you will be welcoming your students into your home for business purposes, your standard homeowners' insurance may not be sufficient to cover your assets in case of an accident. Consult a representative at your insurance agency for complete details on how to ensure that you and your clients are protected in the case of an emergency, big or small. If you rent your home, inquire about tacking additional protection onto your renters' insurance.

Accounting and Taxes

Recordkeeping and taxes will be examined in further detail in chapter 8. However, it's important to keep an eye on these issues from day one so that the systems you

Hot Tip

Remember to save and file all receipts pertaining to business expenses. This will come in handy at tax time and in the unlikely event of an IRS audit.

set up now will facilitate easy and accurate recordkeeping and straightforward tax filings in the future.

Most important, home-based businesses require deliberate efforts to separate personal and business records. Proactive organization not only keeps your business running smoothly, but it also protects your interests. Good organizational habits include:

- Updating all records in a timely and accurate manner
- Saving all business documents in a dedicated folder on your computer
- Color-coding file folders for easy identification
- Learning how to use the functions in your spreadsheet and/or accounting software
- Documenting all incoming money and outgoing expenses
- Retaining all receipts from business-related purchases

As for taxes, this is a complicated issue with diverse ramifications depending on where you live, how you set up your business, and other financial facts unique to you and your household. It's recommended that you consult an accountant for tips on how best to set up your bookkeeping systems from the start. Come tax time, your accountant can take charge and help you comply with all state and federal regulations.

For now, your most critical tax-related task should be planning to set aside 20 to 30 percent of the business's gross revenue to cover your quarterly tax bills. (Your accountant can inform you of the estimated percentage that most accurately applies to your individual circumstances.) When you're self-employed, taxes are not automatically deducted from your paycheck and then adjusted annually through tax returns. Instead, you will have to plan and save for your state and federal tax bills, which are likely due on a quarterly basis. If you make the mistake of considering all business revenue yours to keep, you could find yourself short on cash for Uncle Sam when tax time comes around. Avoid this stress completely by budgeting realistically and setting aside the approximate amount of money you will need for all applicable taxes.

Also ask your accountant for the quarterly due dates for taxes. Pop these deadlines into your calendar and be aware of when they are approaching. It's up to you, with the help of your accountant, to comply proactively and avoid all penalties.

Start your business off on the right organizational foot by deliberately designing systems that will keep you and your business organized for the long term. Then stick

Starting Your Business, Step By Step

Consult with your state's particular requirements for starting a business. The following outline provides a basic guideline to get you started:

- File for a DBA/FBN, if applicable.
- Apply for a business license in your state.
- Set up a business bank account.
- Make sure you and your business are properly insured.
- Save all receipts and maintain an accurate accounting of expenses and income.
- File for quarterly taxes.

to these positive habits day in and day out. Your peace of mind as a business owner depends on it.

Consulting Professionals

Although home-based tutoring is a relatively simple industry (no products to sell, no space to lease, etc.), that doesn't mean you can ignore the intricacies required to set up your business. If certain aspects of setting up the business prove tricky or confusing to you, it's best to seek the help of professionals who can guide you through the process. Ask colleagues and friends for referrals to professionals who specialize in the legalities concerning businesses similar to yours.

So while it's certainly possible to navigate the world of business on your own (armed with this book, a search engine, and a telephone), you may find that you'd prefer to spend a little extra money up front by hiring, for example, a business attorney and/or accountant to support your efforts. Some new business owners value the freedom that comes with not having to be bogged down with entrepreneurial technicalities. For a fee, these experts will take care of the business details so that you can instead focus on building your client base, meeting student needs, and developing your skills as a tutor. If you choose this route, here are some questions and issues you might want to bring up with the experts.

Prepaid Legal Insurance

Did you know that, for as little as $1 a day, you can secure access to attorneys who specialize in your type of business? Prepaid legal insurance entitles you to ask an attorney questions to clarify how you should proceed in certain tricky situations. Additionally, legal services will be available to you in case of delinquent payments, problems with competitors, or any other potential liabilities that come along with owning your own business.

The Business Attorney

Most likely, your business attorney will only need to be involved in the beginning of the process. Home-based tutors should rely on business attorneys for help in complying with local zoning regulations, formalizing a sole proprietorship (or other business structure), and protecting against liabilities. Here are some questions to take to a business attorney:

- How long have you been practicing law?
- What type of business entity should I set up? Can you help me file the appropriate paperwork?
- Do you have experience helping people start small home-based service businesses like mine?
- What are your fees? For what expenses will I be charged?
- Do you have sample legal agreements, forms, and policies available for use in my business?

The Accountant

A trusted accountant can help bring financial security to your endeavor and help you to plan wisely for the future. One of the most valuable assets an accountant brings to the table is knowledge of state and federal tax issues and how you can work within these guidelines to maximize your business's profit and growth. Come tax time, turn to your accountant for help in complying with all applicable regulations and deadlines. Since you will likely have to file quarterly taxes for your business, design a "plan of attack" with your accountant for accurately filing four times per year.

Make sure to choose an accountant with experience and expertise in helping small businesses to start and ultimately thrive. Some of the questions you may want to bring to an accountant include:

- What form of business entity should I establish to maximize my financial well-being?
- Do you have experience helping small businesses like mine?
- What tax strategies do you recommend for my type of business?
- What are my projected taxes for the first year of business?
- When are my taxes due? When do I need to start paying estimated taxes?
- What deductions are available to me and my business?
- What kind of bookkeeping system and/or accounting software do you recommend for my needs?

The Insurance Agent

As the owner of a sole proprietorship, your personal liability is all wrapped up with your legal vulnerabilities as a business owner. That's why it's doubly important to make certain that you and your business are properly insured in the case of unforeseen problems.

Insurance agents can help you secure coverage for comprehensive general liability, accidents, loss of income, health, and more. The main question to ask an insurance agent is: What type of insurance is necessary to protect me and my business? Build the projected costs into your monthly business budget. Reassess your

A Word on Health Insurance

If you are giving up a job that provides health insurance and will thus lack coverage, you should be aware of this potential added cost to your monthly expenses. If you recently left a job, you should procure COBRA coverage which lasts for eighteen months following the date of termination. Ask your business attorney, accountant, insurance agent, or trusted friends for referrals to either a health insurance agent or directly to a health-care provider that works with individuals and small businesses. Sometimes banks offer health insurance services for small business owners.

insurance needs as the business grows and expands. Maintaining a fully insured sole proprietorship gives you the peace of mind to proceed worry-free with both your personal and professional plans.

Printed Materials

Before taking on your first clients, it's a good idea to create specialized printed materials that can help communicate your unique qualifications as an educator, the business's policies, and what clients should expect from working with you. Your Web site will communicate much of this electronically, but consider how the following hard-copy tools can be integrated into your business's operating plan.

Marketing Flyers

In my experience, finding my first clients was as easy as printing up forty to fifty flyers and posting them on the mailboxes around my neighborhood. I included perforated hang tags with my contact information on the bottom, so that interested parties could easily grab my information as they took their daily walks or simply checked the mail. Not very high-tech, I know, but it worked for me, and it might be just that easy for you, too.

No matter how extensive or complex your marketing plan, you will want to design, print, and somehow distribute an informational sheet that introduces you to potential clients, informs them of your services, and tells them how best to reach you. Keep your flyer design consistent with your Web site, résumé, and business cards; this will help you create a recognizable image in the community.

Refer to chapter 10 for a thorough examination of marketing strategies for home-based tutoring businesses.

Business Cards

Business cards are handy marketing tools that fit neatly in your wallet. There are plenty of easy and budget-friendly ways you can design professional-looking business cards.

Try searching the Internet for "free business cards." Many companies offer a small number of free business cards and you can even choose the design. Compare shipping costs and watch out for any "catches" or hidden obligations.

Alternatively, stop by your local office supply store and work with their print and copy center to design your cards. If you're a do-it-yourself kind of person, you can buy perforated blank business cards with preprinted designs. Follow the included instructions and with the help of Microsoft Word and your home printer, you'll have great-looking business cards in less than an hour.

For added coherence, choose a stylistic theme that you can carry throughout your Web site and printed materials. It can be as simple as two to three colors that you consistently use. Your tutoring business sells one product: you. So it's important that you present a unified front that reflects your message and strengths. Avoid any looks that are too flowery or edgy, but instead opt for clean, polished, and professional.

Résumés

Potential clients will want to know that you have the expertise and experience to help them reach their learning goals. You may or may not be asked to provide a résumé to people interested in hiring you, but it's a good idea to have updated copies available to offer new clients. A pithy résumé that lists your training and previous work experience will instill confidence in your abilities to be a successful tutor. On the flip side, a weak, sloppy, or error-ridden résumé could (and should!) be a red flag to potential clients that maybe you aren't the right person for the job.

On a related note, you may want to create an attached list of professional references with contact information. If clients have any reservations about hiring a brand-new business owner for their tutoring needs, being able to make a phone call to verify your professional experience and character could be just the assurance they need in order to give you the green light.

A professional portfolio is an optional tool that can be shown to clients when you initially meet with them. I created a professional portfolio when I sought my first teaching job, so I was able to update it when I began my home-based tutoring business. A portfolio is a binder that presents your résumé, reference letters, licenses, awards, photographs, performance evaluations, and anything else that documents your professional accomplishments.

FAQs for Clients

Consider creating a Frequently Asked Questions (FAQ) document to share with new clients. The list of FAQs can be handed out in hard copy during the initial client meeting and/or posted on your business Web site.

By addressing common questions before they are asked, you will proactively inform your clients about how the tutoring process works and how your business's

Sample FAQs

What is the invoicing process?
What is your late-payment policy?
What is your cancellation policy?
What is your no-show policy?
What is the best way to get a hold of you?
What forms of payment do you accept?
Do you offer tutoring over vacations and summer break?

procedures will look in action. Use this as an opportunity to clarify potential trouble spots (for example, cancellation policies). An FAQ sheet will open up the conversation between you and your clients so that expectations are clear from the start of the relationship.

Tips for Tutoring Success

It's a good idea to provide new students with a list of tips for making the most of their tutoring sessions. Often, younger students don't know exactly how tutors should fit into their academic lives. To address this issue proactively, design a handout of "Tips for Tutoring Success" in which you will suggest how to use the tutor as a resource and partner in the learning process. If you tutor older students or adults, consider adapting the wording to fit your students' needs and concerns.

Building a Business Web Site

The next step in posting an "Open for Business" sign in the metaphorical window of your business comes in the form of a business Web site. Depending on your community, business goals, and personal preferences, you may or may not feel it is necessary to set up shop online. But once you've officially set up the basic business apparatus, it's the perfect time to consider establishing a strategic online presence to showcase your services and what you have to offer. Even if you've never designed a Web site before, it really couldn't be simpler nowadays for Web-site novices to create a simple, professional-looking business Web site that both expresses and furthers your business objectives.

Sample Tips for Student Success

- Ask questions! Don't be afraid to let me know if you don't understand something. That's what I'm here for!
- Complete your homework to the best of your abilities, but don't stress over it. If you come to a problem that you don't understand, give it a try for a minute or so. If you still can't come up with the answer, then circle it. When we meet, I will know to help you with those problems.
- In class, listen carefully to your teacher and take notes. Use a sticky note or other code to flag the concepts that you don't fully understand. Bring these concerns to me at your next tutoring session.
- During the school year, please bring your homework assignments (along with your textbooks) so that I can help it needed.

Using a fun and easy Web tool like Weebly (more on everything Web-related in chapter 11), it can take less than an hour to create a polished Web site that suits your style and your needs. Once you've set up your site, you may be surprised by the various ways it helps you run an effective and visible business. With time, you may even be able to monetize your online presence in creative ways.

For now, consider investing some time in a basic Web site that gets the job done. With so many people now using the Internet to find solutions to all of life's concerns, it's important that your business take its rightful place among the private tutoring options that can be found online by Web surfers in your community.

Ready to Tutor!

Until now, starting your home-based tutoring business has been a relatively solitary and bureaucratic endeavor. Are you ready to meet your future students? I'm excited for you to begin your career as a one-person direct-instruction tutoring machine! All of your preliminary hard work is about to pay off.

06 Home-Based Tutoring in Practice

Because home-based tutoring shares some characteristics with classroom teaching and yet differs in other substantial ways, this chapter may be the most important exploration of the specialized ways you will need to apply your skill set to running your new business. You're no longer representing a school district's policies or a principal's vision; instead, you're the face of a brand-new tutoring business that requires you to put your "best foot forward" from the very start. It's now solely up to you to define the tenor and focus of your professional efforts. Use the next steps in the process to express your confidence and enthusiasm to your new students, and you'll soon feel empowered as both a business owner and as a tutor.

The Successful Initial Parent Phone Call

In many cases, prospective clients will call you at low points in the learning process. It may be a poor report card, a failing test score, or a discouraging parent-teacher conference. Whatever the triggering event may be, you can expect that a caller inquiring about your tutoring services has an outlook that lies somewhere on the spectrum between concern and panic. I've even had parents call me for the first time three days before a final examination, desperately hoping that I could help turn a student's semester grade around ASAP! (In such a situation, I recommend taking a deep breath with the caller, tempering his or her expectations, and, if you're up to a challenge, getting to work right away to make as much of a difference as is realistically possible.)

So while most initial client phone calls hopefully won't be coming from such an extreme perspective, you still want to strike a confident, calming tone in your introductory conversation. Clients are contacting you for guidance and expertise that they can't provide themselves. Thus, your goals in the initial client phone call should center on:

- Briefly introducing yourself, your qualifications, and your teaching experiences
- Explaining how tutoring can help meet learning goals
- Informing the potential client of your hourly rates
- Learning a little about the prospective student (age, grade level, strengths and weaknesses, past obstacles to learning, general learning goals, etc.)
- Setting up the time and date for an initial meeting, if agreeable to both parties

Begin and end the conversation on a friendly, positive note, as you clearly communicate the seeds of an action plan. The call should essentially serve as one part sales pitch, one part introductory meeting, and one part pedagogical planning. With focus and care, your initial client communication will both lessen the caller's worry and increase the chances for a successful tutor-student relationship to begin. When that happens, consider the call a resounding success.

Note: If the client initially contacts you via e-mail, it is still recommended that you set up a phone call to make the communications more personal and welcoming. While a certain amount of introductory information can be effectively shared over e-mail, it is always crucial to establish voice contact at some point before the initial in-person meeting. It will instill confidence and connection in both parties, adding a human touch to what will hopefully evolve into a successful working relationship.

The Initial Parent-Student-Tutor Meeting

At the close of the initial client phone call, you likely arranged for an in-person meeting to occur either at your home or that of the client. A third option, meeting in a neutral public location, might be most appropriate if the client has not yet decided definitively whether or not to utilize your services. Consider a coffee shop or library, among other appropriate sites.

If you will be holding tutoring sessions in your home, the prospective client will likely want to check out your household environment and make sure that it is appropriate and safe for the student. In that case, it's a good idea to hold the initial meeting at your home.

Goals/Purpose

Regardless of where the initial meeting takes place, the goals are similar to the initial phone call, but now you will be taking the interaction to a deeper and more substantial level. In person, ensure that your appearance and manner correspond with the competent professional the client spoke with over the phone. Take this face-to-face meeting as an opportunity to dive into further detail on your procedures, policies, and the specific plan of attack for this individual student's learning goals.

Make a Positive First Impression

It's such a cliché, but a person really does get only one chance to make a first impression. You obviously made it past the first step in the client's screening process—the initial phone call. Your personality, core qualifications, hourly rates, and confident demeanor all presented well over the phone. So, focus on these positives and don't be nervous about meeting clients in person! You are a capable tutor, an empowered business owner, and a true professional who is eager to help students meet their learning goals.

Take a deep breath and imagine yourself as the client meeting you for the first time. What would you hope to see, learn, and sense from a tutor? As essentially the host of this meeting, you set a proper tone with a friendly smile, firm handshake, and an intelligent game plan to meet your new student's learning needs.

Personal Appearance

Make sure your appearance sends a confident, trustworthy message to your new client. Similar to appropriate classroom attire, wear an outfit that is comfortable, modest, and polished. Even if you're tutoring from home, it is not appropriate to wear couch-potato attire to your new job—despite the fact that your commute is a ten-step walk across the living room. Sweatpants or an otherwise untidy wardrobe choice will telegraph to your students that they should treat tutoring sessions casually, and that it's okay to put forth minimal effort when in your presence.

When I tutor, I normally wear a simple pair of jeans with a button-down top that is tailored, but not tight. I apply natural-looking daytime makeup and make sure my hair is combed and usually tied back in a ponytail. If you appear very young, consider putting forth extra effort to present a more mature and thus confidence-inspiring ensemble.

Some of my students are culturally inclined to take their shoes off upon entering my home; in such cases, I follow suit and wear socks. Otherwise, I put on a pair of shoes, even though I don't typically wear shoes when I'm relaxing at home. Jewelry should be simple, and T-shirts shouldn't bear distracting or controversial messages. It's a good idea to follow these same attire guidelines during your initial client meeting.

And while we're on the subject of personal grooming, let's have a word here about the sensitive subject of one's breath. I am always conscious of the fact that one-on-one tutoring places me in extremely close proximity to my students. So I make sure to brush my teeth before my first session of the day, and I keep breath mints in my tutoring supply box. I have this nightmare of a student going home and saying to his mom, "Don't make me go to that stinky tutoring lady's house again! Her breath smells!" So while it's a small and unsavory detail to consider, I do recommend being aware of the various ways that you and your house can appear welcoming and pleasant to your students. Better to be proactive and neutralize any potential trouble spots before they arise in front of students. This goes for the initial meeting, as well as all subsequent tutoring sessions.

Your Tidy, Organized Home (If Applicable)

If you are a mobile tutor meeting prospective clients at their homes or at a public location, your clients may never step over the threshold of your home. Thus, my only home-related advice would be to take note of any potential distractions that may need to be addressed in your clients' homes when you first visit them there. For example, you may need to tactfully talk to the client about putting an energetic pet in the garage during tutoring sessions, or arranging for siblings to stay away from the tutoring workspace for an hour each week. If these types of issues cannot be addressed and resolved, it may be counterproductive to tutor in a particular client's home, and you may need to put an alternative plan in place. Hopefully such issues will be rare, but if they arise, ideally both parties will be ready to compromise in order to resolve them.

In-home tutors, however, will need to put forth concerted effort to present their homes as welcoming, safe, quiet places where learning can easily take place. Parents of young children will especially want to see that your home is:

- Tidy and clean
- Lacking visible materials that are inappropriate for children (i.e., racy magazines on coffee tables, bottles of alcohol, packs of cigarettes, etc.)

- Devoid of religious or political messages that might conflict with their own, or otherwise create an imposing environment for their children to visit regularly
- Safe from aggressive dogs and other potential hazards
- Generally calm, organized, and comfortable

Basically, prospective clients, especially parents of young children, want to see that you are a mature, trustworthy adult who takes life—and work—seriously. What they see in your appearance, personality, and home will speak volumes as to whether they can trust you not only with their children's learning needs, but also with their personal safety.

Professional Preparation

Of course, the primary purpose of the initial meeting is to address a specific learning problem head-on with a custom-designed action plan to be administered by a competent professional. That's you. So beyond the wardrobe and dust bunnies, it's most critical that you spend time before the meeting contemplating the best way to instruct the student and make progress along the learning continuum.

Think in specifics, and prepare notes so that you can effectively communicate your initial thoughts and proposed plan to the client. Pull from all of the instructional methods in your teaching tool kit. Consult colleagues, textbooks, and online resources for creative solutions that could work with this particular student. Additional research will likely be necessary after the meeting (and on an ongoing basis) as you learn more and more about how a particular student thinks and best learns. But for this initial meeting, aim to show off your instructional "chops" so that new clients know they are in good hands.

When speaking to clients, avoid esoteric pedagogical lingo and speak plainly in terms that will inspire their buy-in and confidence. Offer concrete evidence that your proposed methods are proven and effective. Gather relevant textbooks, workbooks, and other materials to demonstrate that you are prepared, knowledgeable, and ready to get to work. Always allow time for the clients to ask questions.

Listen to Parental Concerns

When clients call for help from a tutor, they are often in panic mode, desperate for a professional who will listen to their concerns and help them get out of the metaphorical hole they feel they are currently in. During the initial client meeting, you will likely need to spend a few minutes listening to the clients' worries, or even their complaints. Sometimes they may be looking to hire a tutor because of an incident with their child's classroom teacher, who they consider biased, mean, or downright incompetent. As a tutor, it is not your job to gossip or badmouth other educators. In fact, this can backfire on you and be bad for business. Avoid any temptation to confirm, deny, or commiserate with clients about other individuals that they may blame for their current perceived crisis.

Instead, listen patiently. Then carefully turn the subject back around to how the future will be brighter now that you are working with them to meet specific learning goals. Show concern, but tilt the conversation more toward future success than past failures. While you will want to understand challenging factors that may have compromised learning in the past, your job as the tutor is to be a resource for new solutions and a leader toward a new reality. Your proactive, positive attitude will give them solace (whether they know it or not, at first), inspiring them to rely on your expertise and optimism from the start of the relationship.

Questions to Ask the Client

A key asset that can be gained from the initial client meeting is information about the student's personality and background, school history, and any perceived weaknesses or limitations. By asking key questions of the client (and the student directly, if applicable), you can empower yourself with valuable data that will inform the instructional plan you develop. Some of the questions can be planned ahead of time, while others will arise as the conversation progresses. Here are some core questions that you may want to start with:

- What are the student's favorite subjects in school? Least favorite?
- What factors do you think are contributing most to the problem at hand?
- Are there any other languages spoken in the home? What was the student's first language?
- Is there any history of diagnosed learning disabilities that I should know about? Is the student receiving any specialized instructional support through the school?
- Does the student turn in homework assignments consistently?
- Is the student a strong or weak test taker?

- How are the student's organizational skills?
- What are your short- and long-term educational goals? (Press for specifics on this question.)

Take detailed notes for future reference. Be careful to use neutral, investigative language that assures the client that you are not looking to judge or blame anyone for past problems, but rather, that you are gathering information in order to most efficiently plan for future success. Sometimes, I present the analogy of a tutor as doctor, saying "If you don't tell me where it hurts, I won't know how to fix it." If the client senses an overall friendly and professional "vibe" during the course of the meeting, you will notice their comfort and openness naturally increasing.

Listen to What Is Unsaid

In addition to asking and answering questions, be on the lookout for any subtle undercurrents to the conversation, especially between a student and his or her parents. Your intuition and experience working with families will alert you to potential barriers to student success that the client may not want to reveal explicitly, but are very real nonetheless.

For example, if a student's parents are divorced, you may pick up on a tense schism between each individual parent's approaches, expectations, or behaviors as they pertain to the child's education. Similarly, you may notice that a student's educational background points to grades dropping around the time of the divorce. Although it is certainly not a tutor's business to meddle in family dynamics, the most effective tutors address and support a student's growth holistically. Even if your observation is never spoken aloud, it often cannot be overlooked as a key factor in why a student needs extra support in order to succeed at school.

Determine a Plan of Action

The main value of your business lies in your ability to assess a student's current situation and design an ambitious, instructionally sound plan for meeting concrete learning goals. While telling you how to accomplish this on a pedagogical level is beyond the scope of this book, there are certain common steps that will maximize your power to achieve whatever goals you set, however you choose to proceed instructionally.

Set Specific, Written Goals

In a classroom setting, teachers generally work toward broad, district-determined learning goals that are largely applicable to the class as a whole. Good teachers try their best to tailor instruction toward the needs of individual students, but their effectiveness can be mitigated by the sheer number of students for which they are responsible. The power of one-on-one tutoring comes from the individualized attention that a private tutor offers, in the form of ongoing assessment, personalized instruction, and focused direct attention.

You will flourish as a business owner and as a tutor to the extent that you are able to set, communicate, adapt, and meet the goals you determine for each student. If you are able to delineate three to five specific objectives by the end of the initial meeting, that's great. Tell the client that you will e-mail them a copy of the formal goals within twenty-four hours. If you need additional time to reflect upon what you've learned, simply let the client know your plan. They will respect your thoughtful guidance and expertise. Writing specific goals is a crucial and nonnegotiable part of your business's "product line." It's also an opportunity to show off your pedagogical expertise and demonstrate proactively that you can be trusted to accomplish what you set out to do.

Communicate How Parents Can Support the Plan

No matter the venue, we educators cannot work miracles on our own. In order to maximize efficiency and progress, we must enlist the support of parents, in whatever manner we can get it. It works best to give parents very specific assignments to do on a regular basis with their children. When you ask parents to support the stated learning goals, your suggested tasks should be straightforward and simple, while including materials that make it easy for them to follow through.

For example, practicing multiplication facts with flashcards is something constructive that any parent can do in just five to ten minutes per day. Another idea is to provide a few links to Web sites that the child can use to reinforce key skills at home. Avoid giving busywork, and only assign tasks that you can directly tie to a specific objective that you will also be addressing with the student during tutoring sessions.

If the parents do not follow through in the manner they agreed to, I recommend letting it go. You may follow up with one friendly reminder, inquiring if there's any way you could support them in working with their child. But beyond

Ways that Parents Can Support Learning Goals

- Practicing flashcards daily (five to ten minutes)
- Checking backpacks and notebooks to verify follow-through on new organizational and/or study-skills strategies (five minutes)
- Verifying completion of homework assignments (five minutes)
- Reading books aloud together nightly (twenty minutes)
- Implementing a family reading time to support strong reading habits (thirty to sixty minutes)

that, focus on what you yourself can control—namely, everything that happens during tutoring sessions. It's wonderful when you can count on the parents for complementary support, but in the end, it shouldn't be essential to your success as a tutor.

Agree to a Schedule

One of the most important details to be worked out during the initial client meeting is when the tutoring sessions will take place. If you are already operating from a set schedule, let the client know of any and all available spots you have. If you are starting from scratch and will need to accommodate the schedules of multiple clients, jot down the client's daily and weekly availability. Emphasize the need for flexibility in order to find times that will work well for everyone. You may have to get back to the client at a later date to verify the schedule after you've spent some time fine-tuning it.

Procuring Materials

Once the learning objectives are set and the first tutoring session is on the schedule, think about everything you will need in order to effectively work with an individual student. Each client will require a different set of tools for learning; in fact, that's a main reason that private tutors are hired—for the personalized attention to detail.

Suggested tutoring supplies were listed in detail in chapter 3. Typically, they can be purchased at an office supply store or your local educational materials shop. Other sources for low-cost, high-quality tutoring materials may include:

- Amazon.com or eBay for used textbooks, student workbooks, teachers' manuals, reading materials, and more
- Teachers at local schools who may be retiring and thus looking to give away their stashes of classroom supplies
- Your local library's used-book sales and/or store
- Neighborhood schools who may have surplus textbooks available for sale or loan

The point here is that it doesn't have to cost a fortune to stock your tutoring supply cabinet. Keep an eye out for bargains, get creative, and watch your collection of usable materials grow with time. Every so often, you may have to splurge on a pricey brand-new textbook in order to accommodate a new student's needs. Even if you don't always have the luxury of searching for the best bargain, every item you purchase can be used over and over again to help your students.

I'd like to mention a few other options for procuring supplies, just to give you something to think about. Besides buying textbooks yourself, it may be possible to make a different arrangement with a given client. If their needs are particularly esoteric and you wouldn't be able to use the textbook again in the future, you can opt to clarify that the client will need to purchase and supply any required materials. Of course, after the tutoring relationship is over, the client should keep any of the textbooks.

Alternatively, you can set it up so that you purchase the textbooks and subsequently invoice the client for reimbursement of the full costs. This transaction should be a wash for you at tax time because the cost of the materials counts as both income and a business expense. However, check with your accountant about any ramifications that might arise from this arrangement.

With my home-based tutoring business, I take responsibility for buying all supplies without reimbursement. I consider this a fair part of the cost of doing business. Plus, this arrangement provides me with more control over what materials I use. I appreciate being able to keep all the materials for future use. As I watch my supply of handpicked instructional materials grow, I feel that I am building a cache of tutoring supplies that can meet the needs of almost any student that could walk through my door.

Get Permission to Contact the Classroom Teacher (If Applicable)

One of the most valuable avenues for gaining information about student needs and meeting educational goals is through contact with the student's classroom teacher. Ensure that you have permission from the parents before taking this step. I've never had a parent say no to this request; on the contrary, parents are usually delighted that I am willing to take this extra step to learn about their child and coordinate with the other educators in his or her life. Most schools' Web sites display each teacher's e-mail address and phone number if the parents don't have the contact information handy.

When you contact the classroom teacher, offer a little information about your goals for the student. However, be careful not to venture into the realm of sharing private information about the student or the family. Do not complain or vent. Keep your communication professional in tone and focused on quantifiable learning objectives.

Sample E-Mail to the Classroom Teacher

Hi, Mr. Johnson—

My name is Jane Smith, and I am a tutor in the nearby community. I recently started working with Benjamin Jones as a new tutoring student to help him be more successful in your algebra class. His parents gave me permission to contact you as part of our efforts to help Benjamin improve his understanding and performance. I wanted to touch base with you via e-mail to get any feedback, suggestions, or tips for success in your class that will help me support Benjamin. He told me that he currently has a D in your class. I want to help him do better on his weekly quizzes and tests so that he can earn a higher grade.

Please let me know what you've noticed with Benjamin so far, as well as any other suggestions you might have to help him raise his grade and be successful in algebra this year. Also, does he turn in his homework assignments regularly? I appreciate your time.

Thank you,
Jane Smith

Upon e-mailing the teachers, I have received a wide spectrum of responses. While I have never been completely ignored, I have received anywhere from an enthusiastic bounty of insight and advice to a cursory few words about what skills the student needs to develop. I'll take whatever I can get because I'm mindful that classroom teachers are very busy and I wouldn't want to add to their to-do lists. Sometimes I've encountered teachers at the end of their proverbial ropes with my students. These teachers are almost clinging to me for the supplementary progress they hope I'll be able to make. In such cases, I've found committed partners who are eager to work with me to enhance students' academic success.

Many of my students receive their homework assignments via their school's Web site, so this is another way to make a tutor-to-classroom connection. If they are willing to give me their user names and passwords, then I can log in and check grades, see communications from classroom teachers, and verify homework assignments. This technique has come in handy when I've had a student tell me, "I don't have any homework this week" and I can directly verify this assertion myself.

Communicate Your Policies and Procedures

In order to run a successful home-based tutoring business, it's not enough simply to formulate and codify your policies and procedures. The essential next steps are clearly communicating the guidelines to your clients, and then securing their agreement and buy-in. Standardized rules bring order and equity to client tutor relationships. Naturally, you may have to slightly customize a rule here or there so that you can provide the best service to your clients. Begin with a well-thought-out framework and go forward from that starting point.

Secure Parental Agreement Through a Contract

Putting your policies and procedures into writing can protect you and your business from any misunderstandings or conflicts. This is the perfect project for your business attorney, who can assist you in drawing up an agreement that protects you and your business from any liabilities. When you first meet with a new client, review the policies with them and obtain a signature. File away a signed copy for yourself and provide the client with one for future reference. Beyond protecting your business, a formally signed agreement between you and your clients sends the message that, even though tutoring may happen in your home or that of the client, this relationship is a professional endeavor that requires commitment from both sides.

Sample Tutor-Parent Contract

On Thursday, January 29, 2009, the client ________________________ and the tutor Jane Smith are entering into an agreement whereby Ms. Smith will provide customized one-on-one tutoring services to ________________________. This relationship will begin on ________________________ and continue until either the client or Ms. Smith communicates otherwise. Tutoring services will be carried out in the home of ________________________. Initially, the time of the tutoring sessions is agreed to be at _______ a.m. / p.m. every ________________________ (day of the week).

The client agrees to abide by the tutor's attached policies and procedures. Invoices will be sent by the 1st of each month to the following address: ________________________. Payments shall be due on a monthly basis by the 10th of the month. Late payments are subject to a late fee of $10. Cancellations are also subject to penalty as set out in the attached cancellation policy outline.

As a tutoring client, please be aware that Ms. Smith is always available for questions, suggestions, and consultations. Communication is a key part of a productive, long-term relationship. Ms. Smith's updated contact information can be found on the attached business card. The client can best support the student's progress by responding to all communications in a timely manner.

By signing below, the client and tutor agree to the above terms. Any changes to these terms, if necessary, will be communicated (and agreed to) in writing at a later date.

Date: ________________________

____

Jane Smith

____

Client

____

Student (as applicable)

Some of the policies and procedures you may want to include in any formal agreement include:

- Hourly rate and what it entitles the client to receive
- Invoicing/payment instructions
- Late-payment penalties
- Cancellation policy

At the advice of your business attorney, other elements should be included. Once the policies are explained and formally agreed to, the client-tutor relationship can be built on a foundation of respect and shared expectations. Plus, if there's ever a problem, you can show the client the signed paper to remind them of their commitment to the protocol.

Supplementary Materials for the Initial Meeting

To further your goals of orienting new clients into the business's system and procedures, it's a good idea to provide a few supplementary printed materials at the initial meeting. Preprinted templates will help you organize your thoughts as you ask questions and learn about the student's background and goals, while informational handouts will reinforce your explanations of business policies and procedures.

Initial Meeting Template

Before each initial client meeting, I print out a blank template that I've created where I can jot down everything I learn about my new student on one easy, organized sheet. There's space for basic contact information, background details, answers to my predetermined questions, and any other relevant insight I might gain during the course of the meeting.

Custom Learning Resources Guide

Depending on the circumstances, I may have varying expectations as to whether the parents of a young student are open and able to support our learning goals through at-home efforts in between tutoring sessions. Usually, I err on the side of hoping they will be enthusiastic boosters of the objectives I've set for the student.

Thus, it's a good idea to compile a customized collection of links and easy learning activities that the parent can work on from home. Another useful resource may be a reading list with suggested titles that the parents can purchase or check out

Initial Client Meeting Notes

Date of Meeting: ______________________

Student's name:

Parents' names:

Phone numbers:

E-mail addresses:

Educational background:

Subjects:

Goals:

Questions I have:

Notes:

from the library. I like to present parents with a personalized handout that guides them along an appropriate learning path; even though parents are often willing to help, sometimes they just don't know how to proceed. At the first meeting, you may not know much about what the student needs to learn, so consider presenting them with an initial handout that lists general learning resources, and follow up later with more-customized recommendations.

Adult students may also appreciate receiving an individualized guide to supplementary learning activities that they can do in between sessions. Think about recommending books, Web sites, games, and more. With adults, you cut out the middle man (i.e., the parents) and theoretically have greater odds of participation. It can be presumed that adult students are inherently eager to learn if they have sought out a tutor for a particular subject matter. Why not try to make the most of their enthusiasm and interest?

Web Sites to Suggest to Clients

Of course, nothing can replace the customized, human-delivered learning program that you design and administer to your students. But these fun activities will sneak a little fun learning into their lives in between tutoring sessions. Explore these sites yourself, and you may find valuable resources for teachers, as well.

Elementary

- Free Reading Motivation Program: www.bookadventure.com
- Language Arts and Social Studies: www.timeforkids.com
- Multiple-Subject Games: www.funbrain.com

Middle and High School

- Homework High: www.channel4learning.net/apps/homeworkhigh
- Math Tutorials and Games: www.mathgoodies.com
- Quizzes, Puzzles, and More: www.highschoolace.com

SAT Preparation

- Free Online Prep: www.number2.com
- Official SAT Question of the Day: www.collegeboard.com/apps/qotd/question
- Vocabulary Development: www.freerice.com

FAQs Sheet for Parents

To facilitate clear communication and shared positive expectations, compile a Frequently Asked Questions (FAQ) sheet. Refer back to chapter 5 for suggested questions to include. An FAQ handout serves to anticipate and answer common client questions before they are asked. The client will appreciate having important answers on one handy page. Naturally, you may need to adjust and amend your FAQ sheet as you interact more and more with your client base. There may be other questions or concerns that frequently arise.

Setting Up a Scheduling System

Between multiple families' ballet lessons, soccer games, and piano practices, setting up a master tutoring schedule may be the most challenging part of your new job. When inquiring about a client's daily and weekly availability, politely emphasize the need for flexibility from all parties, including yourself. The more options that clients can give you, the greater the chances that you will be able to find days and times that accommodate everyone's needs and wants. Communicate to all clients that once the schedule is set, there will be little room for changes because any one movement will affect other people as well.

Although determining my schedule at the start of a new school year can be rather tricky, it's always worked out smoothly in the end. Sometimes, in order to make it work, I've had to add days or times to my own availability that I would have preferred to leave blocked off. As a business owner aiming to build a thriving enterprise in the community, I am highly motivated to accommodate any and all clients who are interested in my services. So while it's a good idea to have an "ideal" scheduling scenario in mind from the outset, be aware that the final weekly schedule may look slightly different from the one you envisioned initially. Usually such situations will end up being temporary, as individual situations change or new semesters come and go.

On a weekly basis, I use a hard-copy calendar that I keep with my tutoring supplies for easy access during workdays. Another option would be to use the calendar functionality in your e-mail/contact program. If you keep your laptop nearby during tutoring sessions, you could quickly refer to the electronic calendar and make notes or changes. However you choose to maintain your calendar, remember that your business is time-based, and thus accuracy is of the utmost importance. Create a robust and easy-to-use system that can grow with your business. In home-based

A Typical Day

2:00–3:00 p.m. Perform administrative tasks, such as updating records, generating invoices, communicating with clients, and preparing for the day's students

3:00–3:30 p.m. Tidy up and eat a little "brain food" snack

3:30–4:30 p.m. Tutoring session (tenth-grade geometry)

4:30–4:45 p.m. Break and prepare for next student

4:45–5:45 p.m. Tutoring session (seventh-grade math)

5:45–6:00 p.m. Break and prepare for next student

6:00–7:00 p.m. Tutoring session (eleventh-grade SAT preparation)

7:00–7:30 p.m. Clean up and perform daily bookkeeping

tutoring, your calendar must serve as not only a framework for what *will* happen when, but also to document what *did* happen on a client-by-client basis.

In your calendar, arrange a system to keep track of anomalies such as no-shows and cancellations. I also recommend devising a way to document which students showed up, and for how long. For example, when a student arrives and sits down for a tutoring session, I highlight his or her name in orange on my calendar. It's low-tech to be sure, but when I look back through my calendar, I know that the highlighted names represent tutoring sessions that definitely occurred. Such checks and balances ensure maximum accuracy when it comes time to invoice your clients.

Establishing a Rapport with Your Students

Of course, it's possible for students to learn and succeed under the tutelage of someone they don't like or respect. But isn't it so much easier (and more pleasant!) to create a student-tutor relationship that mixes respect with a dash of fun and levity?

At this stage in the game, you've already built the beginnings of a strong working relationship with the parents (if you are tutoring young children). However, it's just as important to bond with your new students and show them that you are someone they can trust and enjoy working with. Of course, you don't want to take this concept overboard, becoming buddies and compromising your ability to lead and teach. If you've worked previously as a classroom teacher, you certainly know how to walk this line with finesse. I recommend using the following methods to build a positive rapport with your tutoring students. Most of these tips are adaptable for adult students, as well.

Be Frank and Open

Upon first meeting with a new student, see if you can sense any limitations to learning that the student perceives but perhaps didn't feel comfortable saying in front of his or her parents during the initial meeting. If it feels right, delicately broach the subject with the student, perhaps asking, "Why do you think math has become so challenging for you this year?" Or, "Did you ever feel positively about writing?" Listen and express understanding for the student's perspective.

Whether or not you judge the student's perceptions to be valid, it's important to understand how the student feels about what brought him or her into this new tutoring relationship. Keep any revelations in mind as you design your instructional plan. Most often, my students tell me that they felt positive about a given subject for many years until they fell behind in the work, or began to sense that their classmates were more competent at the coursework. To me, this is good news, because I can help them achieve success fairly quickly, building up their confidence, which often leads to a better overall attitude about the class.

This attitude of openness can also flow in the other direction; show your human side and let your students know about difficulties you had in school with particular subjects. Offer insight as to how your outlook changed and what tools you adopted in order to ultimately find success. Students of all ages may naturally feel intimidated by mentors who appear perfect or for whom everything seems to come easily. Putting your fallible side on display (mixed in with practical lessons for how to overcome common roadblocks) is a surefire way to help students relax and trust you as a mentor and expert.

Offer Encouragement

Often, by the time a student reaches the point of turning to a tutor for help, he or she has already become demoralized and discouraged, whether by a parent's visible disappointment or a perceived slight by a classroom teacher. Low test scores and poor grades often immediately precede hiring a tutor, so you may have to do some work rebuilding a student's confidence alongside the academic assignments at hand. This can be accomplished in a variety of ways, including:

- Pointing out evidence of the student's strengths (in a certain subject or in school generally)
- Explicitly celebrating even the smallest successes, whether it be turning in a homework assignment on time or earning a passing score on a quiz
- Giving compliments when the student answers any question correctly
- Providing the student with the tools to gain competence in a given subject area
- Sharing your own experiences of feeling challenged or overwhelmed in school, and how you worked your way out of it
- Telling the student about positive comments made by his or her parents or classroom teacher

Keep in mind the all-important theory of the self-fulfilling prophecy. In my teacher's education courses, we were told that if a teacher believes that children can learn, the children will sense that confidence, start to believe in themselves, and achieve learning goals beyond expectations. As a personal tutor, you are in a uniquely intimate position to effect this kind of positive change in the lives of your students.

Session Notes

Don't rely on just your memory to help you guide your students toward the progress you have planned for them. With multiple students and sometimes up to a week in between tutoring sessions with an individual student, it's easy to forget where you left off during the last session and where you wanted to go in the next one.

Avoid this problem by jotting down notes during and/or after each student's session, for future guidance and reference. Write down problems you noticed, concepts you need to reinforce, learning activities that you want to do next, and any other observations (big or small) that you need to remember in the short and/or long term. After each session, take a moment to reflect on the progress made and any ideas you have for the next steps. Then, file your notes in the student's file (in chronological order, ideally). In between sessions, follow up on outstanding action items, if any. For example, you might need to communicate something specific to the student's parents, or purchase a teaching material that will further your objectives for that student. Before the next session, take out the previous session's notes for review, to help you plan the next set of lessons.

Sample Template for Tutoring Session Notes (by Student)

Today's date: ________________

Date of next session: ________________

Student's name: ______________________

Observations/notes:

Homework assigned (due next session):

Ideas/plans for next session:

Action items (before next session):

Personal Touches for Creating Happy Clients

- Remember birthdays
- Celebrate good grades on quizzes, tests, and report cards
- Show them you can understand or relate to their concerns
- Be fair and believe in your students' abilities
- Go above and beyond the call of duty
- Share a little about yourself, when appropriate
- Smile, laugh, and be human

Consistently following this routine will help ensure that nothing falls through the cracks, as you juggle multiple students and all of the details that come along with running a business. This will also free up your mind to stay in the moment without having to keep a running list of things to remember all day long and throughout the week.

Show Your Personality

Teachers and tutors are at their most powerful when they are well-rounded, wise instructors. By bringing your multidimensional personality to the tutoring table, your students can come to not only trust you, but admire you.

For example, my students know that I love football, reading, cooking, and everything Japanese. I can use bits of these topics in sample questions that I design or to illustrate academic points. This helps my students think about how academic material can be creatively linked to their own interests, hobbies, and experiences.

Throughout the course of a tutoring session, I often weave in little stories from my own school days to show how I can relate to problems they are facing and that it's possible to come out on the other side of challenging classes or a rough school year. I can tell this helps my students view me as someone who has "been there" and understands. I am careful not to overindulge my own life stories to a captive audience, and so I quickly reroute the discussion back to the schoolwork at hand. But I believe that sharing your passions, life experiences, and idiosyncrasies with students is a fun shortcut to a warm working connection, especially in the beginning of the student-tutor relationship.

Find Commonalities

As humans, we are more alike than we are different. Thus, I find it possible to uncover commonalities with each and every student, no matter how different we may seem on the surface. Recognizing shared interests goes a long way toward making a student feel comfortable in my home and in my presence. I would never want a student to feel uneasy or intimidated by the tutoring experience, so I bridge the gap between student and tutor by integrating examples from our shared likes and dislikes into the work.

For example, if I know that both I and my student are San Diego Chargers fans, I could create a word problem along the lines of, "If LaDainian Tomlinson runs the 40-yard dash at 18 miles per hour, how many kilometers per hour is that?" If you are an engaged and energetic educator, it's probably second nature for you to forge these types of connections with your students. I'm grateful that one-on-one tutoring affords a plethora of opportunities to connect with students in this personalized way. It makes the whole experience more fun and enjoyable for all.

Dovetail with the Classroom Teacher's Style

It's only natural that every instructor teaches in a unique style and explains basic concepts in a distinct manner. But as a tutor, you do not want to complicate a student's learning process by trying to piggyback a completely different vocabulary or solution method onto the way it's being taught in the classroom. As I work with my students, I listen to how they explain the concepts being taught and try to use the same language they have picked up on through other teachers' explanations. I take notes and mimic the classroom teacher's methods and terminology as best I can.

For example, one student's teacher calls the distributive property of multiplication "spreading the love." If I tell my student to distribute a number while solving an algebra problem, he hesitates and loses track of the steps. However, if I prompt him to "spread the love," he flows smoothly through the solution, and we even share a little chuckle over what a silly expression that is.

Most of the time, you will be able to naturally pick up on the language of the classroom teacher. If you have a copy of the textbook, that will also offer some guidance. But remember: You can always directly ask the student, or even the classroom teacher, about instructional precedents. The important thing is to streamline learning for the student and minimize extraneous information that just convolutes the educational process.

Real-Life Example: A Typical Tutoring Session

With so many methods and styles of tutoring available, one can imagine that there's no such thing as a "typical" tutoring session. Besides, each individual tutor brings a unique personality and approach to the job, which is what makes one-on-one instruction so valuable and effective.

Still, let's examine a core framework to guide you in designing a one-hour tutoring session for your business.

Ninth-Grade Algebra In-Home Tutoring Session (4:00–5:00 p.m.)

Welcome (4:00–4:05 p.m.)

- Greet student, welcome into your home, and get settled
- Inquire about recent grades and upcoming quizzes or tests
- Ask if the student perceives any challenges or concerns (get details)
- Review any previously assigned work that is now due

Direct Instruction (4:05–4:20 p.m.)

- Deliver direct instruction on material currently being worked on during class
- Provide time for student questions

Session Memo

One easy and effective way to communicate to parents about the progress made in a given tutoring session is through something I call the Session Memo. I print out a stack of half-page sheets with a blank template that I can fill in at the end of each tutoring session. It only takes me a minute or two to complete, but it helps show the parents that valuable learning takes place during each and every meeting. An example of a sample session memo is on the next page.

A Note from Mrs. Smith

Student's name: ______________________________

Date: ______________________________

What we worked on today: ______________________________

Next time we'll work on: ______________________________

Homework assignment (due next session): ______________________________

A Note from Mrs. Smith

Student's name: ______________________________

Date: ______________________________

What we worked on today: ______________________________

Next time we'll work on: ______________________________

Homework assignment (due next session): ______________________________

- Offer study tips and test-taking strategies specific to material at hand

Guided Practice (4:20–4:45 p.m.)

- Give the student problems to solve that reflect the concepts from today's direct instruction
- Watch closely for repeated errors and immediately address any misunderstandings
- Re-teach any concepts that still need reinforcement

Closing (4:45–5:00 p.m.)

- Preview upcoming concepts to facilitate understanding
- Offer brief enrichment activities to get ahead, if appropriate
- Assign independent practice questions to be completed by the next tutoring session
- Fill out a Session Memo and give to the student (with directions to give it to the parents)

Ongoing Client Updates

If you are tutoring young children, you need to cultivate a positive relationship not only with your students, but also with their parents. By being a proactive, problem-solving communicator, you will set the tone for a happy and likely long-term relationship with your clients.

A tutor should never live by the motto, "No news is good news." Instead, your business will flourish through your proactive attention, communication, and creative solutions. If parents don't hear from you on a regular basis, you risk having them make the assumption that nothing positive is being accomplished in the tutoring sessions. Why should they pay you for tutoring sessions when no apparent progress is being made?

Former classroom teachers probably have already mastered how to communicate problems to parents. It requires a delicate mix of practicality, support, and optimism. Similarly, private tutors should only contact parents with a problem after they have quantifiably assessed student progress, identified impediments to learning and areas for growth, and then devised a research-based solution. Following these steps with care and sensitivity will help parents to trust your expertise and the tutoring process.

Typically, I communicate with parents through e-mail, over the phone, or in person when they come to pick up the child. I highly recommend e-mail because it creates an automatic paper trail that documents your exact words. Also, in-person conversations at the door during pickup time tend to get lengthy, and thus infringe upon the flow of your daily work schedule.

No matter which form of communication you use, the most important factors to get right are consistency and regularity. Consider making a checklist to help you keep track of when you speak to each client. I wouldn't recommend going more than two weeks without speaking to a client about how things are going, unless it is vacation time.

When I invoice my clients monthly over e-mail, I make sure to include a few sentences at the end that address what I am observing with the student, how I think the parents could support learning at home, and how I plan to work with the students to achieve improvement. Always assure clients that you are available for any and all questions, and that you appreciate the opportunity to work with them.

If you are not tutoring young children, then it is presumed that the client and student are one and the same. Thus, you will likely be able to effectively communicate assessment information and instructional plans within the context of a tutoring session. I still think it is a good idea to summarize this information in e-mails on a regular basis. Not only does this serve as written documentation in case of a

Ways to Retain Clients

- Deliver quantifiable improvements (for example: higher grade point average).
- Communicate clearly and proactively (on issues both big and small).
- Demonstrate that you enjoy working with the student.
- Find and implement the perfect mix of fun, discipline, and high expectations.
- Offer outstanding value through highly customized, quality instruction.
- Explain what you are doing and why (and how you know it works).
- Be consistent and fair in enforcing policies.

disagreement, but it also gives the student/client another opportunity to process the big picture in a quiet setting on his or her own terms.

Keeping Clients Happy

It is just as important to retain "old" clients as it is to attract new ones to your business. With time, you will develop a friendly camaraderie with your students. Even better, you will be able to anticipate their needs and understand how their minds work as you function together as a learning team. And, to be honest, veteran students often require less preparation time (compared to brand-new students) because you know what to expect from your tutoring sessions, you develop a routine together, and you can sense how to make direct progress with them because you know them so well.

All of this is just to say that, as your business grows, one of your top priorities should be to keep your current clients happy. It makes your job easier, builds a positive reputation for your business in the community, and allows you to maximize your instructional efficiency.

Personal Touches

Hopefully, one of the reasons you entered teaching is because you love working with people. It should come naturally to you to develop warm, friendly, personal relationships with your students. Similar to classroom teachers, tutors can share their distinct characters with students as a key tool for building rapport. As students get to know your individual nature (quirks and all!), they will enjoy working with you and buy into the tutoring process more fully.

Another way to bring a personal touch to your tutoring business is through remembering student birthdays, acknowledging holidays, and celebrating learning

Web Sites to Help You Tutor

Graphic Organizers: www.eduplace.com/graphicorganizer
Multiple Subjects: www.discoveryeducation.com
Reading: www.beyondbooks.com
Writing: www.webenglishteacher.com

successes. So, if you've been working hard to help a student pass her Spanish final examination and she earns an A on the test, it's a good idea to mark the occasion in some small way, such as a card, short e-mail, or a sweet treat. Keep in mind that young students often crave kudos from their parents above recognition from anyone else, so you can hook them up by bragging directly to the parents about their hard work and accomplishments. That little bit of outside praise can go a long way toward creating goodwill between child and parent (and parent and tutor, as well).

07 Financial Planning and Management

Two of the most attractive features of a home-based tutoring business are the low start-up costs and the minimal ongoing expenses. By definition, you don't have to rent space for a store, you aren't selling a product that you must keep in stock, and virtually all of the materials you purchase can be used over and over for years to come.

Still, all savvy business owners must plan a strategy for managing incoming payments, business expenses, quarterly taxes, and more. In addition, policies such as a cancellation clause may have financial ramifications that must be accounted for. And, crucially, you must proactively address the most fundamental potential drawback to being a private tutor—the yearly school calendar ebb and flow that can result in dry summers and flush autumns.

With proper planning and sound management skills, the financial side of your home-based tutoring business will flow smoothly and efficiently. This allows you to focus your energies on what matters most: helping students reach their learning goals.

Factors to Consider When Setting Your Hourly Rate

Here's my cautionary tale on setting hourly rates. When I first started out as a home-based tutor, I was eager to get off to a fast start by attracting as many clients as I could in a short time. This outlook came back to bite me when I realized that I had set my rates too low for my region and skill level. By the time I had a full docket of clients, I was happy to be working and helping my new students, but I felt trapped by the low rates that I had used to jump-start my business. I felt that to raise the rates after the fact would be unfair to my clients and could potentially alienate them from me and my work. I wasn't willing to risk this negative outcome, so I kept these low rates for over two years!

After I realized that I had sold myself short, I adjusted my rates for all new clients, keeping the hourly rate thoroughly reasonable but slightly more in line with what other tutors were charging in the community. This change helped me feel that I was earning a rate that was commensurate with the value I was bringing to my clients' learning lives.

So I learned an important lesson from all of this, and I hope you will benefit from my mistake. Don't sell yourself short. It's not always best to aim for quantity or speed at the expense of devaluing your own professional worth. While I didn't enter private tutoring primarily for the money, it still didn't feel good to know that I had done a financial disservice to myself from the outset. I quickly came to enjoy my work and my students so sincerely that I was intrinsically motivated to go the extra mile for them, regardless of financial compensation. However, I think it's important to set a fair, reasonable price for your services and then focus on the instructional progress you can make, which is where the real job satisfaction will come.

Check Out the Competition

I've had many initial phone calls from prospective clients where they mention that they've already investigated the rates and services offered at a nearby corporate tutoring center. Due to large-scale marketing campaigns, these centers are often the first place parents turn when panic starts to set in after a poor report card or a gloomy parent-teacher conference.

I've found that if I can set my hourly rates slightly lower than these corporate centers, almost all prospective clients opt to go with the more-individualized, homespun option (i.e., me and you). As home-based tutors, we're kind of like the mom-and-pop stores of the private tutoring world. It feels more comfortable, intimate, and direct to work with a professionally trained tutor that lives down the street, as opposed to a fluorescently lit franchise that follows decrees from a faraway corporate headquarters.

Investigate the larger-scale tutoring options in your community, knowing that parents may often call there first. Once they have had an initial encounter with the corporate tutoring center, your friendly and casual expertise may seem like a breath of fresh air. And if your rates are competitive with (but perhaps slightly lower than) those of the corporate center, then it seems like a no-brainer to me!

Another avenue for price comparison lies in the rates charged by other local tutors in your community. By comparing what similarly trained tutors are charging for comparable services, you can then arm yourself with key information that will help you set your prices accordingly. You can't exactly call the other tutors and pry directly; after all, this is your competition in the marketplace. But by searching online bulletin boards (for example, Craigslist), you can discreetly gain insight into what various private education services are going for in your community.

The wisest way to set reasonable rates that will attract quality clients is to:

- Do your research
- Honestly assess your value
- Be aggressive, but perhaps flexible

Although setting your hourly rate can easily become a task fraught with tension and worry, just remember that no matter what your compensation, you are serving your community through your expertise and positive intentions. Even if you come to feel that you initially erred in setting your rate, this mistake can easily be amended with time as you come to better understand the marketplace. Ultimately, the marketplace plays a major role in determining the rates you can charge in your community. So while I shared my cautionary tale of setting a rate too low, I still believe it's better to price your services competitively and get your feet wet with your new business than to be waiting by the phone for clients who are put off by your prices. The wisest way is to do your research, get started, and reassess with time.

Issues to Explore When Setting Your Hourly Rate

What do the corporate tutoring centers charge for one-on-one instruction?

What are other local tutors charging for your preferred grade level and subject matter?

What unique qualifications or certifications do you possess that add value to the instruction you offer?

How many quality references can you offer?

Should you charge varying rates depending on the age of the student or the subject matter being taught?

How many years of experience do you have?

Designing and Enforcing Your Cancellation Policy

Without a formal cancellation policy agreed to by client and tutor, your business lacks a certain formality and mutual respect. Even the most well-intentioned clients could take advantage of you if there are no consequences for their actions. Late cancellations and no-shows affect the bottom line of your business's financial well-being. Your time is valuable and should be respected, just as you make sure to be timely and ready to work for each tutoring session on your schedule.

Your cancellation policy should reflect a firm yet reasonable approach. You aren't aiming to punish clients for extenuating circumstances that inevitably arise a couple of times per year. Rather, your cancellation policy serves to express a disincentive for clients to casually cancel tutoring sessions at the last minute for nonemergency reasons.

New clients should be informed of the cancellation policy at the initial meeting. You can secure their formal written agreement via the tutoring contract, as discussed in chapter 6.

When a client cancels a tutoring session, you may use your discretion as to whether you will charge them for the cancellation or not. For example, I can't envision myself charging a client that called me from the emergency room with a child's illness, or if there is a death in the family. Again, the cancellation policy exists to

Sample Cancellation Policy

A scheduled tutoring session may be canceled at least 24 hours in advance without penalty. Cancellations within 24 hours are subject to the following penalties:

$10 for the first late cancellation

50 percent of the hourly rate for the second late cancellation

100 percent of the hourly rate for the third late cancellation

"No shows" without a phone call will be required to pay 100 percent of the hourly rate.

All reasonable extenuating circumstances will be taken into account. Repetitive late cancellations and/or "no shows" may result in termination of tutoring services.

protect you and your business from frivolous cancellations. As you get to know your clients, I think it will be clear which clients are being thoughtless and require the full enforcement of your policy and which clients are sincerely in need of your case-by-case understanding.

Weathering Seasonal Ebbs and Flows

Private tutoring of school-aged children typically revolves around the local school district's annual calendar. When school starts, the business tends to pick up. During vacations and summer break, your average weekly hours could wane or even stop completely.

That's why it's crucial that you be strategic in your efforts to make the most of year-round tutoring opportunities. With a little creativity, you can create a steady revenue stream that continues to flow even during the seasons when you might otherwise be twiddling your thumbs. Without a proactive approach, you may find that your September through June tutoring income isn't enough to support your household's economic commitments throughout all twelve months of the year. This is where sound financial planning comes into play for you as a business owner.

When I worked as a classroom teacher, the school district offered the option of receiving an annual salary in ten, eleven, or twelve monthly payments. Even though we were only contracted to work roughly ten months out of the year, we could elect to receive paychecks even in the summer months. That way, our income was automatically spread evenly throughout the year.

Typical Recurring Expenses

- Paper
- Textbooks and workbooks
- Toner for printing
- Web-hosting and domain-name fees, as applicable
- Writing utensils

Unfortunately, there's not such an easy solution when you own and operate your own tutoring business. You will have to devise your own solutions for realistically anticipating monthly income levels and spreading the sum throughout the year. That way, your high-season income levels will carry you through the off-season with comfort and ease.

One solution is to use your business bank account as an automated budgeting tool. You can put all of your tutoring income earned throughout the year into your business bank account, and then make arrangements with the bank to transfer a given monthly amount into your personal accounts for household use. Work with your accountant to calculate how much money you need to set aside for quarterly taxes, and leave a base amount to cover any business expenses. After subtracting these costs from your estimated annual income, divide the remainder by twelve, and that's how much should be transferred to your personal account each month. With this system, you can count on a certain monthly income level from your tutoring business which makes it easier to plan accurately in your personal life.

It is naturally challenging to plan your annual income for the very first year of business. With time and experience, you will be able to more accurately gauge how much the business will bring in annually. To start off, err on the lower end of the estimated spectrum. That way, you'll avoid overreaching and depending upon money that may not pan out.

(In chapter 10, we will explore innovative ways to create a thriving year-round market for your business by maximizing off-season tutoring opportunities.)

Invoicing

The invoicing process is the bread and butter of your company's financial well-being. It's important to set up an organized invoicing process, secure each client's agreement by contract at the initial meeting, and then implement the policy accurately

Hot Tip

Visit www.OpenOffice.org for free office software that allows you to read and write Microsoft Office documents in a smooth and powerful interface. OpenOffice comes with a one-button PDF export function that creates easy, e-mail-able invoices.

Sample Invoice

Tutor Name

Business Name

Tutor's Address

Tutor's Phone Number

INVOICE

INVOICE #133

DATE: 8/27/09

TO:

Client's Name

Client's Address

Client's Phone Number

FOR:

Tutoring Services

DESCRIPTION	HOURS	RATE	AMOUNT
Reading and Writing Tutoring Services for Benjamin (February 1, 2009–February 28, 2009)			
• February 15, 16, 22, 23 (1 hour each)	4	$35/hour	$140.00
		TOTAL	$140.00

Make all checks payable to Tutor's Name

Total due within 10 days.

Please note:

No-shows, late cancellations, and late payments are subject to the penalties outlined in the tutoring contract.

Thank you!

and consistently. Documentation is the key to avoiding misunderstandings that could lead to conflict.

Your spreadsheet software offers invoice templates that can pull data from a spreadsheet and synthesize it into a standardized invoice format. This document can then be printed and sent (or e-mailed) to the client. Try searching for "Service Invoice" in Microsoft Excel.

Schedule

I invoice my clients via e-mail on the first of each month. In my opinion, any more frequently would result in a burdensome level of bookkeeping, and any less frequently would not make financial sense as a business owner. I prefer using e-mail to invoice my clients because it keeps all transactions and communications documented and saved in one easy click. I arbitrarily chose the first of the month for invoicing because it is an easy time for all parties to remember.

A few of my clients prefer to automatically bring a check for me every four lessons. I am willing to accommodate this arrangement, but I am careful to manage it through detailed records. Although it is a little more work for me to accommodate a whole separate invoicing schedule for just one or two students, I try to make it work for these long-term, loyal clients. It is up to you whether you are okay with having more than one invoicing schedule up and running at a time. Just make sure to accordingly amend the tutoring contract at the beginning of your relationship with that particular client.

Method: Paper vs. E-mail

Perhaps you and/or your clients prefer to take the invoicing process off-line and use hard copies. If that's the case, prepare the printed invoices before the appointed invoicing date, place them in envelopes labeled with each student's name, and make sure to hand the invoice to the client at the next tutoring session. With this system, it may not work to invoice on the first of each month, for example, because that date won't always correspond to when you see a particular student. Delineate the plan in the client contract to avoid misunderstandings.

To compare the two methods, e-mail invoicing saves paper, while providing automatic documentation, immediacy, and opportunities for communication. E-mails aren't as easily lost as paper invoices. However, if you have clients that never

Monthly Log for __________________

Tutoring Sessions

Date	Student Name	Day/Time	# of Hours

Money Received

Date	Student Name	Check #	Check Amt.	Notes

(or only sporadically) use e-mail, it is certainly possible to make hard-copy invoices work well within the structure of your business.

Hot Tip

All incoming cash and checks must be documented through your bookkeeping system and deposited into your business bank account. Streamline the process through QuickBooks (or similar accounting software) that can be set up to automatically synchronize with your bank. That way, any bank deposits will be itemized and logged into your accounting software with just the click of a button.

Final Word on Invoicing

All of these choices are ultimately up to you as the owner of your business. The only nonnegotiable factors are consistency and communication. Once you and your clients agree to a certain procedure, it's up to you to follow through on the expectation of consistency with timely and thorough action. Demonstrated integrity and attention to detail will showcase your business as a legitimate entity to be respected in the community.

Budgets

The process of setting a budget can be both enlightening and formative for your business's development. By taking the time to thoughtfully estimate your expenses and income, you set up the business for success from its inception. With time, you will gain more insight into the intricacies of your home-based tutoring business and become more accurate at formulating your monthly and yearly budgets.

To start, use the Budget Template below to project monthly income and expenses, making adjustments that reflect the practicalities of your own business. Gather quotes and perform research so that your estimates are as accurate as possible. Approximate your revenue by calculating your billable hours per month multiplied by your hourly rate. After the monthly budget is made, you can then extrapolate an annual snapshot that will give you a picture of the yearly financial outlook for your business. As your business develops and perhaps adds structural

Sample Budget Template

Jane Smith Tutoring Services			Projected vs. Actual Monthly Budget	
Expenses	**Budget ($)**	**Actual ($)**	**Difference ($)**	**Difference (%)**
Advertising				
Dues and subscriptions				
Gas (mobile tutors only)				
Health insurance				
Instructional materials				
Legal and accounting fees				
Liability insurance				
Office supplies				
Postage				
Taxes				
Telephone				
Web-related				
Other				
Total Expenses	**Budget ($)**	**Actual ($)**	**Difference ($)**	**Difference (%)**
Income	**Budget ($)**	**Actual ($)**	**Difference ($)**	**Difference (%)**
From tutoring sessions				
Other				
Total Income	**Budget ($)**	**Actual ($)**	**Difference ($)**	**Difference (%)**
Balance	**Actual Income**	**Actual Expenses**	**Difference ($)**	**Difference (%)**

complexities, your budgets will become more involved as well. Establishing strong budgeting habits now will enable your business to expand according to your long-term vision.

So while the financial side of a home-based tutoring business is inherently rather straightforward when compared to more complex businesses, there are clear consequences to taking shortcuts with effective money management. No one should become a tutor simply for the cash, but it's a wasted opportunity to give short shrift to the business's profit potential. Aim to strike the perfect balance between financial savvy and pedagogical passion, and you'll be guiding your business down a rewarding professional path.

08 Recordkeeping and Taxes

Bookkeeping and taxes were discussed briefly in chapter 5 when we examined how to officially set up your business for growth and profitability. These issues are the cornerstone of running a business that meets your financial needs. Without appropriate tools and processes in place, you may be setting yourself up for not only unnecessary work and expense, but perhaps even legal troubles and stressful tax audits. That's why it's best to arm yourself with information, be meticulous in maintaining your records, and proactively comply with policies that keep your business running like a finely tuned machine.

Recordkeeping

Hopefully, you've already been deliberately separating your personal and business records. Working from home, it can be all too easy to blur the lines between family resources and work materials. But with a little proactive organization and discipline, your business will function smoothly while simultaneously protecting your interests. Other good organizational habits look like this:

- All records are updated in a timely and accurate manner.
- All business-related electronic documents are stored in a dedicated folder on your computer, separate from personal items.
- File folders are color-coded for easy identification.
- Spreadsheet and/or accounting software functionality are utilized effectively.
- All incoming money and outgoing expenses are properly documented.
- All receipts from business-related purchases are saved and filed accordingly.

Hot Tip

Remember to back up your business-related computer files on a regular basis! There's nothing more frustrating—or time-consuming—than having to re-create months (or even years) of business documents lost in a computer glitch. Set up an automatic backup system so you don't even have to think about it.

Software Solutions

There's nothing wrong with keeping your books by hand with old-fashioned paper and pencil tools. If that's what you're comfortable with and it suits the needs of your day-to-day operations, go for it.

But you may instead be interested in harnessing the power offered by electronic spreadsheet and accounting tools. Even if you've never used a particular software program before, it won't take much time to play around with a program, get familiar with the functionality, and customize the settings to meet your business needs. This initial time investment will pay dividends throughout your tenure as a business owner because the right software setup saves you valuable time, hassle, and maybe even money with regular, disciplined use.

If you're already an experienced user of spreadsheet software such as Microsoft Excel, it may make the most sense for you to go that route. Otherwise, explore accounting-specific software such as Intuit QuickBooks. Software options are discussed in more detail in chapter 3.

Bookkeeping in Practice

Once you've decided on a bookkeeping system, take some time to customize it to meet your unique needs. There's no need (or benefit) to using the one-size-fits-all, out-of-the-box settings if they convolute or otherwise don't fit your operational procedures and preferences.

For a home-based tutoring business, it likely makes the most sense to organize your books by student for easy reference and individual tracking. You'll also want to make a master file that reflects the business operations as a whole; this may include dated listings of all incoming revenue, outgoing expenses, and money to be put aside for projected taxes for a given quarter or fiscal year. If you've opened a separate business bank account, you can log on to your account through your bank's Web site and get at-a-glance reporting of the actual balance and account history. This can be an important tool for double-checking the accuracy of what your accounting or spreadsheet software reflects.

Consistency is Key

Even the most meticulously organized bookkeeping framework can be made obsolete by lack of attention from the business owner. It's crucial to devise and follow a regular routine for maintaining accurate business records. Don't rely on your memory and vow to do large-scale data entry at a later date. Instead, set yourself (and your business) up for success by documenting business transactions on a daily or, at the very least, weekly basis.

Sloppy and/or inaccurate records are the surest route to business chaos. And whether you're aware of it or not, such slacking will inevitably show itself, in one way or another, to your clients. Careful accounting isn't necessarily glamorous or fun, but it's a critical factor in running a smooth and all-around successful business—both behind the scenes and in front of clients.

Flexibility = Strength

If, as your business evolves, you discover new snags in the system that need to be ironed out, you may choose to add new organizational solutions to your routine. Each person, business, and household presents unique circumstances that need to be managed proactively; otherwise, you run the risk of your systems turning into problems with time, especially with the added complexity of integrating a business into the home. Aim to design robust bookkeeping systems that can grow and adapt as your business evolves. That's the surest way to build a strong foundation for your business, both now and in the future.

Hot Tip

Save and file all receipts from business purchases. This will save you money during tax time, and in the unlikely event of an IRS audit.

Mobile Tutors: Keep Track of Miles

If you will be driving to tutoring appointments, keep track of any miles driven for business purposes to facilitate tax write-offs. At your local office supply store, you can buy a small booklet to keep in your car, specifically for documenting miles. Although the deduction may not be large, every bit of savings helps.

Taxes

Unless you are a certified accountant or otherwise familiar with applicable tax codes and regulations, it's always a good idea to consult an accountant whose expertise can help you set up and run your business in the most fiscally responsible way. (Refer to chapter 5 for recommended questions to ask prospective accountants.)

Independent of the relationship with your accountant, it's a good idea to arm yourself with basic tax information that gives you an overview of how things will work with your new home-based tutoring business. If this is your first time being self-employed, it can feel unfamiliar to take such a hands-on, proactive approach to your taxes. Know that deductions are no longer automatically withheld from your paycheck, as was the case when you worked for someone else. For that reason, you will want to set aside 20 to 30 percent of the business's income to cover tax bills. Consult an accountant to verify that this recommended percentage applies to your individual financial circumstances. It is likely that you will need to file taxes on a quarterly basis (not just annually on April 15). Be aware of all state and federal deadlines so that payments and paperwork can be filed in a timely manner.

FYI

The U.S. tax code is rather strict when it comes to writing off an area of your home for business purposes. You only qualify for the deduction if you regularly use an area of your home *exclusively* for business. The area must also be the principal location of your business or the place where you usually meet with clients.

If you set up your business as a sole proprietorship, you will be filing your business and personal taxes together on one return. Known commonly as "pass-through" taxation, this uncomplicated procedure is considered advantageous to small business owners because the ultimate tax burden is often less than it would be with double taxation. Simply fill out a 1040 form, along with a Schedule C which breaks down the profit/loss for a business.

09 Ethical Issues

As the public face of your tutoring business, the most valuable asset you possess is your reputation. Your image in the community rises and falls based on the quantifiable results you deliver, as well as how you express a sense of integrity and fairness through business relationships. Essentially it boils down to what you do and say (and sometimes, more importantly, what you *don't* do or say).

The cultivation of a strong, positive reputation doesn't end when you secure a new client, or even after tutoring sessions begin. Be assured that new clients will be keeping an especially close eye on your words and behavior in the beginning of the relationship. But they will stick with your services for the long haul only to the extent that they feel they can trust you—both professionally and personally.

This chapter explores the dos and don'ts of serving your community as an ethical tutor and business owner. If you have worked previously as a classroom teacher, you may already be adept at avoiding some of the sensitive issues that can arise. However, you will also need to be aware of some potential pitfalls that are unique to home-based tutoring.

Confidentiality Issues

As a private tutor, you are hired as a professional in whom clients can confide their struggles, concerns, and dreams. This channel of honest communication must remain open in order for you to be able to do your best work. It informs your lesson planning to know about problems with classroom teachers, learning disabilities, changes in home life, and other issues that may have had an effect on a student's achievement in the past.

But as parents and students speak to you about their concerns and personal issues, you should start from the premise that all information will be treated sensitively, and considered "for your ears only." You may even want to assure your clients that you will not share their insights with anyone else, particularly the student's classroom teachers (if you choose to contact them).

Some types of sensitive information may include:

- Learning disabilities
- Opinions on a particular teacher's competency level
- Health problems
- Family dynamics (as described to you or as observed by you)
- Grades and test scores
- Psychological concerns
- College admission information
- Religious views

Dos and Don'ts for Ethical Tutoring

Do:

Be overly cautious with sensitive information

Keep most personal opinions (especially political and religious views) to yourself

Imagine how your home environment might appear to visitors

Assure parents that you will treat their confidential information with respect

Be respectful of the customs and viewpoints of your clients

Stay out of any disagreements between your clients and other third parties

Don't:

Share your opinions about other educators or leaders in the community

Take your clients' viewpoints personally

Engage in gossip

Repeat any information or insight shared with you by clients, unless you have the client's permission

Complain to clients about anything (instead, focus on solutions)

Any written notes or documentation pertaining to sensitive issues should be treated with care and stored in your locked confidential business filing system. Password-protect your computer and any electronic files, as necessary. In conversation with other clients, students, or members of the community, be constantly mindful that your words carry weight, and anything you say could be repeated many times over by people who have little reason to treat the information with care.

If you have children of your own who attend school with your tutoring students, you will need to make extra efforts to safeguard confidential client information that they may not know to keep to themselves. Discuss with your children that they should not repeat anything they may overhear during in-home tutoring sessions. They should not read your confidential files or have access to your business e-mails. While young children most likely would never intend to cause harm to others by repeating information, you can imagine how problems could be caused inadvertently. It's better to be safe than sorry and avoid any potential trouble spots.

Maintaining Neutrality on Sensitive Subjects

There are a few subjects that everyone knows should be avoided at dinner parties, unless you want to invite controversy, tension, and hard feelings. Subjective topics, such as politics and religion, are even more radioactive in the context of an intimately interpersonal business like home-based tutoring.

Whether you visit your clients' homes or invite students into yours, it's best to keep touchy subjects out of the equation altogether. A policy of neutrality is especially good business if you tutor young students. Parents of young children need to feel that they can trust you to care for their kids without asserting undue influence on their easily molded minds. If their children return to them spouting unfamiliar religious doctrine or edgy political slogans, that's a sure way to alienate clients from your business. It should go without saying that any comments related to ethnicity or culture should be treated with similar care (i.e., avoid them completely).

If you host tutoring students in your home, you may also want to be aware of the messages that your decor sends to visitors. Political themes may be visible to students through magazines lying on coffee tables, magnets or stickers hung on a refrigerator, or books on your shelves. Religious beliefs may be communicated in a variety of ways, from publications, wall hangings, or books.

While it would be unrealistic and unnecessary for anyone to expect that you wipe your home clean of your personality and preferences, you might want to consider whether any visible items might make a new client nervous upon first visiting your home, as they imagine dropping their child off with you for an hour or two each week. As the clients get to know you as a tutor and as an individual, they may grow increasingly comfortable with any given situation, especially as they learn that you are avoiding any opportunities to proselytize or moralize. But in my opinion, it's generally a good idea to examine your home with fresh eyes and aim to make a warm, but neutral and nonthreatening, impression upon your clients.

If you are working as a mobile tutor and entering various clients' houses, be respectful of their beliefs and customs. For example, some clients are culturally inclined to remove their shoes upon entering the home. It would be unnecessarily rude to keep your shoes on in this situation. If you see political or religious messages that clash with or offend your own sensibilities, don't take it personally, and certainly don't start an argument. It's not worth damaging your business's prospects and reputation just to make a point. Since your clients are not tutoring business owners, it is not fair to expect them to change their homes and routines to accommodate your short-term presence. It's up to you to bring a flexible, neutral, and professional demeanor to each and every tutoring session. That is what's best for your business (not to mention your mental health!).

Aside from politics and religion, another touchy subject is classroom teacher quality. Sometimes parents contact a tutor at a time of intense frustration with a child's school or a particular teacher. They may be in full-on "rant mode," desperate for a sympathetic ear to which they can vent. While it is your job to listen with care, it benefits no one to hear a long list of complaints. After you've gotten the gist of the situation, gently tilt the conversation back toward the present moment and how you can help the student reach future goals. Even if you possess independent information that would support or deny the client's claims, it's best to bite your tongue for fear of exacerbating an already-tense situation. This approach extends to discussions of any other figures in the community, such as school administrators, corporate tutoring centers, and most especially other private tutors with whom you may compete.

Another scenario that could arise in the course of a tutoring relationship is a student mentioning his or her private opinions of a parent's actions. For instance, a student might complain to you about a parent's decision to send the student to one school or another, or even a divorce or remarriage. To avoid getting in the middle of parent-child squabbles, it's best to maintain a neutral outlook, say as little

A Quick Story

During a recent presidential election, several of my teenaged students asked me for whom I'd be voting, both during the primary and the general election. For over a year, this was a hot topic in the country, and I had to be constantly on my toes to make sure I was maintaining total neutrality in my professional relationships. Even when it was clear that the student and I were in agreement, I still kept my opinions to myself. You never know if parents hold a different opinion, or whether they'd appreciate another adult in the child's life opining on politics without the parents there to mediate. It was a sensitive time for many people, and I felt that I was doing the best thing for myself and my business if I kept my opinions totally to myself. Sometimes it was challenging, because my young students were educated and engaged, looking for someone with whom to discuss their developing ideas. Nevertheless, I chose not to indulge my own ego and my personal passion for talking about politics, and I'm glad I made that choice.

as possible, and move the lesson back to the academic subject at hand. Absolutely never badmouth the parents or their decisions. Trust the parents, stay out of the situation, and do the tutoring work for which you were hired.

Ethical Communications with the Classroom Teacher

When contacting a classroom teacher to form a cooperative partnership, only include general information and pertinent facts. This will typically mean just the student's name, grade level, name of the course being taken, any broad concerns and goals, and the grade you have been told the student currently holds in the class. That way, you are clearly identifying the student in question to a busy classroom teacher with dozens (if not hundreds) of students. You are also aiming to verify the student's current grade and asking for any tips or insight the teacher can offer. Assure the teacher that you have secured the parents' permission to initiate contact. Avoid commiserating with the classroom teacher over the challenges that a certain student presents. Don't assume that the teacher already knows about any learning disabilities, household problems, or the like. You wouldn't want to be the one to share sensitive information that was told to you in confidence. (In chapter 6, you can find a sample e-mail showing how to contact the classroom teacher.)

Business Ethics

Beyond performing as an ethical tutor, there's a whole other moral standard that comes along with owning a small business. This comes into play with how you keep your word with clients, how you report your income to the IRS, and how you bring an honest approach to every part of your business transactions.

Integrity

Just as in friendships, clients appreciate being able to count on you to communicate honestly and follow through on your word. This can take many forms throughout a given day, week, or even year. You can show your clients that "your word is your bond" by:

- Keeping all appointments and minimizing cancellations
- Maintaining confidences
- Communicating any problems or concerns in a timely manner
- Clearly defining your expectations for the relationship and holding all parties accountable
- Being timely with all scheduled invoicing and other routine tasks
- Keeping an open mind to any suggestions or concerns brought up by clients
- Finding opportunities to sincerely praise student achievement and progress
- Treating your clients and students the way you would want to be treated
- Making the most out of every tutoring session, minimizing wasted time and distractions

People get frustrated when they don't know what to expect out of a relationship or situation. Take this potential pitfall out of the equation by approaching your business relationships with an honest, straightforward, and respectful attitude. Think about what you would like and expect if you hired a private tutor, aiming to give your clients and students the best you can at every opportunity.

Finances

When you're in charge of everything financial for your own business, it can perhaps be tempting to fudge numbers or let indiscretions slide. You may even be able to get away with it for a while. However, you will always know about these dishonesties, which will eat away at not only your self-respect, but also your ability to function with integrity in your relationships. Plus, the truth always catches up with people, and the embarrassing consequences of ultimately getting caught will mar your reputation as well as your ability to make money in the future through your home-based tutoring business.

Instead, take the high road and express your personal integrity through your company's finances at every turn. The following actions will help you build a solid foundation for a business built on truth and self-respect:

- Set fair market prices for your services
- Meticulously document all tutoring sessions (noting cancellations, in particular)
- Accurately invoice clients in a timely manner
- File all necessary paperwork to run a business in your region
- Follow all applicable business laws
- Document and report all income received and money spent
- Comply with tax codes (both state and federal) and pay your taxes in a timely manner

To Sum Up

The old adage "It's better to be safe than sorry" certainly applies to the realm of home-based tutoring business ethics. Imagine the regret you would feel if one slip of the tongue drove loyal customers away from your business and compromised your livelihood. It may sound dramatic, but it's best to manage your business with caution and prudence in all areas. As a home-based tutor, not only are you inviting clients into your home (or entering theirs), but you are also working one-on-one with students whose trust and confidence you need to earn and regularly renew. Always be mindful of the fact that your reputation will be built through your interpersonal skills, particularly tact and discretion.

10 Marketing Your Tutoring Services

Effective marketing makes or breaks any business. You could offer the world's best tutoring services, but it won't matter a bit if you can't get the word out and attract customers. Alternatively, your tutoring services could be mediocre, and by putting on a confident, classy face, you could be booked to capacity in no time. I certainly wouldn't recommend following the second example, but it just goes to show how crucial a strong and well-executed marketing plan can be to a new business. Potential customers will make their decisions based on the image you present, and they'll only find out about your business if you think objectively about how best to reach them.

Your ability to market your business will also be what gets you through the ebbs and flows that naturally accompany a tutoring business. Through proactively implementing creative marketing strategies, you can turn slow summers into busy and profitable seasons that keep your balance sheet moving in the right direction year-round. When you wisely advertise your tutoring services, you increase your visibility in the community, which may lead to innovative new opportunities for growing your business. Your marketing strategy may rely on posting paper flyers, or on Web sites with optimal search engine power. Whether you go high-tech or old-fashioned, it's up to you to utilize the marketing tools that make the best sense for your particular situation.

Marketing Research

Any good marketing plan begins with solid research. While you can perform a good portion of this research through intelligent online searches, that will only take you so far. Consider supplementing your Web-based research with face-to-face conversations with people in the community who fit the demographic that would hire a tutor. Think outside the box and make phone calls

Market Research Basics

What is the state of the market in my surrounding community?

Who are my competitors?

What are the trends?

What kinds of people hire tutors in this community?

What age ranges and subjects are most commonly needed?

Where can I find a high concentration of potential customers?

Are there any unmet needs that I could fulfill?

How do interested potential clients most often search for tutors?

to local experts; one creative information source might be the local school secretary or guidance counselor, who could tell you what type of help parents most often seek for their children. Contact nearby corporate tutoring centers to see if you can glean any information about how they have positioned themselves in the marketplace.

Take notes, ask questions, and then design follow-up questions that expand on what you have learned. Cultivate relationships that will help your business take root and grow. The market research stage is your opportunity to arm yourself with information and to become an expert in your new industry. The more you learn, the more comfortable you will get with the surrounding community and your business's place within it. This will assist you in making the most of any opportunities that may arise, as well as help you streamline the marketing strategies you are about to design and implement.

Marketing Factors

Before you even set foot out of the house to start spreading the word about your business, it's important to ponder your surrounding community, the services you'll offer, your personal financial needs, and your household's lifestyle requirements. You'll also need to consider how you'll best be able to connect with potential customers in your surrounding community. Through realistic planning, a marketing plan will begin to take shape in your mind, which you can then put into action with

How Will You Stand Out in the Marketplace?

Examine your unique strengths and experiences to see how you can make your tutoring services stand out in the crowd. For example, I once worked as an instructor for a major test-preparation company, so I knew that I could zero in on the SAT test-prep market in my surrounding community. Assess your expertise and find specific skills that you can highlight to your advantage through marketing materials.

confidence and gusto. So before you fire up the marketing machine, assess the following issues with honesty and foresight.

How Flexible Are You Willing to Be?

There's a fine line between being accommodating and signing yourself up for a situation that conflicts with your stated business goals. For instance, if you do proper research and set your rates at a certain level, does it make any sense to then lower the rate slightly if a new client calls and inquires about a rate reduction? This compromise may or may not make the difference in attracting that particular client, but you also run the chance of regretting the fact that you sold yourself short from the start. Before the calls start flowing in, take some time to decide where you will be willing to compromise, as this will help you design marketing materials that reflect your true goals and intentions.

Before you begin receiving calls from prospective clients, be clear in your own mind as to whether you are willing to compromise your rates if asked. It's fine either way, but this is something you should think about beforehand so that you can avoid feeling pressured in the moment of an actual phone call. With a little forethought, you can feel in control of the situation rather than put upon.

Rates

We already explored in chapter 7 how you should go about setting your hourly rates. However, this issue also relates to the world of marketing, because competitive rates will ensure that you won't be left out in the cold when potential clients are calling around to compare various tutoring options in the community. Unless you offer extremely specialized expertise that will be highly valued in your particular marketplace, it is probably a good idea to position your business to compete strongly with other available tutoring options. Potential clients will naturally be evaluating the quality of instruction that you bring to the table, but if they decide your business's quality is essentially the same as a competing tutor, it may be your hourly rate that causes them to opt for one of your competitors.

If you can demonstrate a specific added value that you bring to the table, you may feel comfortable pricing your services slightly higher and taking any associated risk. For example, if your competition has a bachelor's degree while you have earned a master's degree in a subject relevant to your tutoring services, you are likely justified in adding a few dollars to your hourly rate. Or, if you are formally trained and experienced at SAT test preparation, you may be able to charge slightly higher rates and still find plenty of interested clients who can more thoroughly trust your expertise.

Location

Before you set up the business, you spent some time honestly reflecting about how best to design your services. But now that it's time for marketing your tutoring business and finding real, live clients, take another moment to consider whether you are willing to compromise on where you will perform your duties. If you've decided that mobile tutoring will mesh best with your lifestyle and needs, what will you say if a ready-and-willing client calls and is unable, for whatever reason, to host the tutoring sessions in his or her home? Will you stick to your guns, or could you compromise in order to gain a client and help a student in need?

Schedule

Scheduling is the main area where compromise will be necessary in order to attract clients and begin productive tutoring relationships. When you begin marketing your business to the community, you should already have an ideal schedule in place that reflects your personal preferences and needs. However, be careful not to come across as too rigid about this ideal schedule when designing your marketing materials or speaking to new clients on the phone. For example, let's say that you write on your marketing materials: "Tutoring available from 3:00 to 6:00 p.m., Monday through Thursday." If a student is only available from 5:30 to 6:30 p.m., he or she might decide not to even bother calling you for more information, assuming you aren't able to work with their schedule. If instead you word it to say, "Tutoring available afternoons, Monday through Thursday," you will increase your chances of

Cautionary Tale

About a year into my career as a tutor, a mother called me in a panic about her son being poorly prepared for an upcoming final examination in math. It was only a week before the final and the mother only told me that the course was called Algebra. Since I often tutor students in this subject, I figured that I could easily help this student raise his grade even in the short amount of time available. It wasn't until the student turned up for the first tutoring session that I realized this was for the second year of algebra (which is really more like trigonometry), and not the first year to which I was accustomed. I hadn't laid my eyes on this particular material since I'd been in high school myself! And to make matters worse, the student already had a B in the class and merely wanted to improve to an A. So in actuality, he knew way more about the subject than I did in that moment! This was the most stressful situation of my tutoring career, and I had gotten myself into this mess all on my own.

Ultimately, I regrouped and turned this scenario into a major positive in my life as a tutor and business owner. After the final examination I continued to work with the student on a weekly basis. I purchased the textbook (and a solutions manual) and completed the course's homework on my own and alongside the students in the class. Essentially, I taught myself the material a few days before each tutoring session so that I was always a few steps ahead of my student. This wasn't the easiest way to learn the second-year algebra material, but the intense work I did meant that I very quickly added second-year algebra to the list of subjects I am qualified to teach. Nothing like a little trial under fire!

What I learned from this intense experience is to ask more questions and take more time before I commit to a new client. If I had asked more questions about the course, I could have learned that it was a subject beyond my qualifications and knowledge base. The parent only knew to call the course "Algebra," and I made the assumption that it was a particular type of algebra. Worst of all, I let the parent's anxiety and urgency affect my response. Sensing the parent's distress, the teacher in me wanted to do anything I could to help. As a result, I put myself in an awkward and challenging position that could have potentially damaged my business and my reputation as a capable professional.

Morals of the story:

Ask questions. Take your time to reflect upon client requests. And never let a parent's frantic tone dictate your decision-making process.

receiving inquiries. Coordinating schedules with five or ten different clients is one of the messiest parts of the job. Your flexibility will enable you to accommodate and ultimately help more students, so make sure that your marketing materials reflect that desire to cooperate.

Ages and Subjects

The ages of your students and the subjects you tutor may be the least flexible areas of your business. After all, if you only know math up to first-year algebra, you simply can't market yourself as a geometry expert or a calculus guru. This issue also ties into age range, naturally. If you are trained as a primary-grade reading instructor, you may not be qualified to (or comfortable with) deviating from that niche.

In your marketing materials, make sure to list absolutely every age and subject you are qualified and willing to teach. No detail is too small, as you just might leave out something that would inspire a potential new client to pick up the phone. As much as possible, list the relevant training and work experience that will back up your claims. This will inspire confidence that you can do what you say you will do, even before the clients speak to you.

If a client calls and inquires about your ability to tutor an age or subject that you didn't anticipate, it's best not to commit to this right away. Ask if you can take a day or two to think it over. Do your research. Perhaps borrow materials from the library, or ask the local school librarian if you can browse through the class textbook. This will help to ensure that you are, in fact, comfortable with the material. After you've gained insight on precisely what the course or subject entails, then you can get back to the client with confidence and professionalism.

Where Will Parents Look for a Tutor in Your Community?

Imagine that you are a concerned parent in your neighborhood who just learned of your child's failing math grade. You decide to look into hiring a private tutor. What would be your next step? Depending on your community, the first step could be an online search, in which case you may want to center your marketing strategy on a polished Web site and a formidable presence in the top search engines. If you decide to use the Internet as the cornerstone of your marketing strategy, refer to chapter 11 for a thorough discussion of how best to make that happen.

In most circumstances, there are low-tech, low-cost ways that potential clients will begin to search for a tutor. One is approaching professionals at the student's school for advice and recommendations. This could mean the classroom teacher, guidance counselor, or office staff. To make the most of this avenue for referrals, introduce yourself to the relevant educators at nearby schools with students of your targeted age group. Offer them a stack of your business cards and/or informational flyers with contact information. These simple steps will maximize the number of referrals you get from these educational pros that parents often turn to in times of worry.

If you are tutoring school-aged students, a common source of client referrals will be your neighbors, the network of parents in your community. Parents talk. They share their concerns and what's worked for their families when they are waiting in the carpool line, shopping for groceries, or even walking around the block. Make sure that your neighbors know about your tutoring business, what services you offer, and how to contact you. Once you have successfully tutored for one family, word will likely spread, and your phone will start ringing more and more. New clients will trust their friends and neighbors who have had positive experiences with you and your business. So treat every client as a potential billboard for your business, because your current clients are the most valuable marketing tool you have. Best of all, they'll spread the word of your services for free!

Where and When to Market Your Business

Where and when you market your business in the community will vary depending on your target market and the goals you set for your business. You may decide to start with the simplest approach, and if that doesn't gain any traction, you can always expand your marketing efforts from there. You may be pleasantly surprised by how easy it can be to share the news about your business through low-tech, homegrown methods.

To begin strategizing about how best to market your business, consider the following questions:

- Where do potential clients most often search for information?
- How can I present a capable, trustworthy image to the public through my marketing decisions?
- What is my marketing budget?
- Where do my target clients frequently gather?
- How can I efficiently reach the greatest number of potential clients?
- When is the best time to market my business? How will that affect my marketing decisions?

When?

Although it may sound strange at first to discuss timing when it comes to marketing your business, if you are tutoring school-aged children (or even college students), home-based tutoring naturally takes on a season-oriented rhythm.

Consider this: Imagine you want to tutor second graders in reading comprehension. Would it make sense to market your services in the middle of July, when students are on summer vacation? I contend it does not. Many families are more school-oriented during the regular school year, preferring to take the summers off from classes and extra obligations. Of course, with some serious searching and a little luck, you could certainly find a few students who are interested in remedial summer catch-up tutoring. However, even in these cases, I would recommend marketing to find these types of students in the final weeks of the school year. Parents like to plan ahead, and, no matter what, are more "in the market" for tutoring services when their children are actually in school mode.

Best Times to Market Your Business

Depending on the type of tutoring services you offer, consider the following guidelines as you plan on when best to market your business.

K–12 (all subjects)

The first week of school

The week of parent-teacher conferences

When progress reports and semester report cards are released

Remedial Summer Work

The final two to four weeks of the school year

The last month before school starts

SAT (or other standardized test preparation)

The three to six months before the most common test administrations

The final two to four weeks of the school year (for students who want to use the summer to prepare)

On the flip side, if you keep track of when parent-teacher conferences occur and semester grades are released, you can time your marketing efforts to reach parents who have just received concrete results about a child's progress in school and what is needed to succeed. Consult each school's online calendar for these important dates. You could even give a few select classroom teachers a stack of your flyers and/or business cards for distribution at conference time or Back to School Night.

You can imagine that there are certain times of the school year when parents have a heightened awareness of their children's progress at school, and thus are increasingly motivated to take action. I recommend building your marketing plan around these occasions if you plan to tutor school-aged students.

If you are tutoring adult students who are not in school, there may not be such a seasonal quality to your work. However, you can still observe the people in your target market and take note of any patterns or trends that you can then factor into your marketing plan. For example, perhaps you live in a region with particularly harsh winters. You may notice that people are less inclined to leave their homes at certain times of the year. Or maybe college-aged students scramble for private tutoring help just before midterms and final exams. It's best to be informed and realistic about the tendencies of your potential clients so that you can plan ahead financially and strategically for your business.

Where to Market

- Distribute printed flyers
- Shared mailboxes
- Door-to-door
- Community bulletin boards
- Library
- Coffee shop
- Community centers
- School front office
- School guidance office
- Printed ads
- Community newsletter
- School newsletter

Where?

By researching your target market, you can become an expert in their behavior, preferences, and needs. This will be particularly helpful information when it comes to deciding

Does your child need a TUTOR?

There's no need to struggle all year long—
I'm a credentialed teacher with immediate availability

- Just a few remaining spots for fall tutoring
- Credentialed multiple-subject teacher
- Trained and tenured in Brookside Unified
- Ivy League–educated
- Nine-year resident of Brentwood community
- Experienced, personable, and goal-driven professional
- Strong communication, results-oriented
- Coordination with classroom teacher
- Experienced teaching new SAT format
- Free initial consultation

- Subjects include:
  - Language Arts
    - SAT skills & techniques
    - Reading (all levels)
    - Writing strategies
    - Spelling skills
  - Math
    - SAT skills & techniques
    - Algebra
    - Geometry
    - Elementary math
  - Study Skills

- 6+ years of K–12 teaching experience
- Neighborhood references available

Contact Jane Today

Call or e-mail for rates and availability

northcountytutor@tutormail.com

555-3254

Tutoring => Confidence => Success

Jane: Credentialed Tutor
555-3254
northcountytutor@tutormail.com

Jane: Credentialed Tutor
555-3254
northcountytutor@tutormail.com

Jane: Credentialed Tutor
555-3254
northcountytutor@tutormail.com

Jane: Credentialed Tutor
555-3254
northcountytutor@tutormail.com

Jane: Credentialed Tutor
555-3254
northcountytutor@tutormail.com

Jane: Credentialed Tutor
555-3254
northcountytutor@tutormail.com

Jane: Credentialed Tutor
555-3254
northcountytutor@tutormail.com

Jane: Credentialed Tutor
555-3254
northcountytutor@tutormail.com

My Simple Marketing Story

Since I live in a close-knit, school-oriented suburban community, I kept my marketing plan deliberately simple from the start. I figured that if my basic beginning strategy didn't yield results, I could always expand my vision from there. But since I had lived in the neighborhood for over five years, I felt that I knew my neighbors' habits pretty well. I started by printing up about fifty marketing flyers with precut hang tags on the bottom. That way, interested parties could easily tear off my contact information as they walked by. I posted the flyers on the shared mailboxes around the neighborhood, timing my efforts to coincide with the nearby elementary school's recent parent-teacher conferences. And that was enough to get my tutoring business up and running! I got several phone calls very quickly, which eventually resulted in a few more client referrals. I didn't have to put much more effort into marketing ever again because word-of-mouth kept my business strong and growing.

where to spend your marketing dollars. After all, it doesn't do any good to place your advertising materials where clients will never encounter them, right?

Creating a Market for "Off-Season" Tutoring

Just because the business of private tutoring often takes on a seasonal rhythm, that doesn't mean you have to go with the flow and accept dry spells as an inevitable part of the package. With proactive planning, you can create off season tutoring opportunities that not only keep your balance sheet moving in the right direction, but also add value for your clients.

Once or twice a year, take a "big picture" look at the calendar and try to anticipate when your business might slow down. If you tutor school-aged children, this might be largely due to school vacations and summer break. If your students attend a year-round school, your slow times may not be as long or severe as those associated with a traditional school calendar. Similarly, if you work with adults who are not enrolled in school, you may be able to maintain a steady pace all year long without any extra effort needed.

But if you're staring at a few dry spells scattered throughout the year, there are several ways that you can mitigate the effects on your business's bottom line.

Cultivate Current Clients

Obviously, it's easiest if you can schedule additional tutoring hours with clients that you already have. If you can come up with a concrete and quantifiable goal for a given student, the client may be interested in using breaks from school to help the student get ahead and reach that goal with your help.

For instance, in your communications with the classroom teacher, it may become obvious that the student has fallen behind in a particular subtopic of a course (i.e., plane geometry of a math course). With the classroom teacher's support and copies of a few failed exams, you can speak to the client about your concern over this issue and offer a detailed plan of attack that could be accomplished over the course of a school vacation. Especially with a course like math, where the material is taught sequentially, it's true that students should be careful not to fall behind, or else they will struggle for the rest of the school year, if not for years to come. Communicate this fact to parents in combination with a concrete plan of action and you may be able to drum up additional business.

Also, keep in mind that some high schools give incoming students summer assignments that they must complete before the first day of school. These projects can be complex and time-consuming, and students often benefit from additional guidance to help them get organized and motivated to complete the work at a high-quality level. Rather than having to spend the summer nagging their child to work on readings and homework, it may very well be worth it for parents to hire you to serve as the taskmaster and supervisor for any projects.

Other areas where you can expand your services to current clients may include standardized test preparation, such as the PSAT, SAT, SAT Subject Tests, and high school exit examinations. Sometimes students who are applying to attend private schools must take a particular aptitude or entrance exam, so that might be another avenue to pursue with certain students.

Find New Recruits

If you've already exhausted any innovative off-season tutoring options within your current pool of clients, you may opt to search for new clients to add to your roster. These new clients could come on board on a temporary basis, or you may be able to convert what was at first a vacation-only arrangement into a more-permanent relationship.

Key Marketing Tools

- Business cards
- Marketing flyers
- Business Web site (paired with Google AdWords)
- Craigslist (and other online message boards)
- Online advertising
- Professional résumé
- List of personal and professional references

One idea is to network with the classroom teachers at a local school to see if you can maximize any potential opportunities with students who are recommended (or required) to attend summer school for remedial purposes. It is likely beyond the school's confidentiality boundaries for them to provide you with a list of summer school students, but perhaps you could give your business cards to certain classroom teachers for distribution to students who can't afford to take a summer vacation from learning.

11 The Internet and Home-Based Tutoring

Nowadays, it's so easy to build a simple business Web site that there's really no reason to skip this effective business-building step. Anyone can make a Web site with a few easy-to-use tools. Did you know that it's no longer necessary to write complicated code in order to design a professional-looking site that represents and furthers the goals of your business? Now is the perfect time to jump into the online world of Web design with both feet. The time you invest in designing a Web site now will pay dividends with time.

Even if you don't plan to market your services online, your business can still benefit from establishing a basic online presence. You can use your Web site to refer potential clients for additional information, showcase your success stories, allow members of the community to contact you easily, and present a polished public face for your business. With proper search-engine optimization, you can get listed in top search engines for free and spread word of your services with minimal costs and effort.

Characteristics of Effective Web Sites

- Simple layout
- Clean, attractive graphics
- Cohesive color scheme
- User-friendly, easy to navigate
- Full of useful information

Building a Business Web Site

Even if you think that your business doesn't need an online presence, consider some of the positive aspects that can come of it. Some of the benefits of having a business Web site for home-based tutoring include:

- An additional path to attract new clients through search-engine results
- A centralized location where you can delineate your vision, available services, policies, and procedures
- A convenient way for students and clients to communicate with you
- An efficient method for happy clients to refer others to your services
- A venue for compiling and sharing your recommended study tools, learning links, tips for success in school, and other helpful resources for your students

Even if you've never created a Web site before, there's no need to be intimidated by the task. As with all technological issues, the most important thing is to be calm and curious, while not getting easily intimidated by the prospect of learning new skills. Remember that you can play around with Web design tools without any risk of breaking anything (and every choice can be undone with no lasting damage). It's so easy now to design a polished online presence that reflects your professional image to the community. You don't even have to know how to write code anymore! Of course, you could hire a Web design professional to make your Web-site dreams a reality . . . for a price.

But if you seek a relatively simple, quick, and completely doable solution, I recommend one of my favorite Web sites for the job—www.weebly.com. If you know how to click, drag, and type, you can have an organized, informative site in the course of about fifteen minutes.

Play around with the site's tools and see if it might fit your needs. You can even buy a domain name through Weebly (or try GoDaddy.com) to reflect your business name. Then set it up so that your new URL forwards to your Weebly site seamlessly. If you want to see a sample of a home-based tutoring Web site made through Weebly, check out the one I made at HiScoreTutoring.weebly.com. I timed it and it took me about forty-five minutes to make.

There may be other similar Web sites out there that can help Web design novices get the job done. Explore, ask friends, and see what's out there. Or, consider trading your tutoring services for Web design favors from a tech-minded friend. (Note that another popular Web design option is Dreamweaver, published by Adobe.)

Why I Recommend Weebly.com

- It's free, and it takes less than an hour to make a functional Web site you can be proud of.
- You can buy a domain name and point it seamlessly to your Weebly site.
- It uses a simple drag-drop-and-type interface that won't intimidate even the most novice Web designer.
- You can customize it with your choice of clean, professional layouts.
- For a simple informational Web site, you don't need to pay good money for a fancier site.

Web Design Tips

Before you start working on your own Web site, take a quick spin around some of your favorite sites and take notes on what you like and don't like about the designs. Search for other home-based tutoring business sites and see what you can learn from the competition (even if they're located across the country or around the world).

I think what you'll observe is that the most effective small-business Web sites offer a clean, easy-to-navigate design expressed through a cohesive color scheme. It's better to keep the look simple than to pile too many bells and whistles into it. The site should be full of updated information that potential and current clients will find useful and relevant to their lives. Your contact information should figure prominently, as well as a basic introduction to your business and a summary of your qualifications and services. You may want to include a photograph of yourself on the main page. If you do add a picture, make sure that it is professional-looking and not of poor quality. Instead of listing the contact information of professional references on the site, I recommend simply writing "References available upon request" at the bottom of an appropriate page. I doubt many of your references would want their personal contact information out there for all to see. Plus, it's best for you to be aware of who's interested in calling your references, so that you can manage the process and be informed of what's going on.

Essentially, you want to use your Web site to present a polished, mature, and trustworthy face to the world. Include enough information to assure potential clients that you are capable and available, but not so much information that potential clients no longer feel the need to contact you directly. The Web site should be informative, but it should leave potential clients eager to talk to you in person and get the process started. Don't make promises you can't keep, but do send the message loud and clear that you are qualified, competent, and ready to work hard for your students. Aim to strike a balance between too little and too much, too meek and too cocky. Ask a friend or family member to read through your site with neutral eyes

Items to Include on Your Web Site

- One photograph of yourself
- Introduction of yourself and the services you offer
- Résumé
- List of subjects and grade levels you tutor
- Available days and hours
- Your educational philosophy
- Testimonials from satisfied clients
- Contact information

Items NOT to Include on Your Web Site

- Rates and other financial details
- Contact information for your references
- Your street address
- Names, pictures, or other identifying information about individual students (past or present) without proper permissions

before you hit "publish." Always consider how your site will appear to Web users who don't know anything else about you and your business. Just as in off-line life, there's only one chance to make a first impression.

Search-Engine Optimization

Similar to the classic adage about a tree falling in a forest, it doesn't do much good to build a functioning business Web site that potential clients can't easily find. That's where search-engine optimization comes in. This refers to the techniques you can use to maximize your site's visibility in top search engines. With a few simple tricks, you can move your site up the search-engine ranks and increase the number of potential clients who view and ultimately visit your site.

Keyword Phrases

The most important search-engine optimization technique is to write powerful titles for each page. The title information that you write will show up to users in the upper left corners of their browsers. Search engines use this information to know what a Web page is about and to help it match the users' searches with the content on each of your Web pages.

The first step to an effective Web page title is to choose a competitive keyword phrase that reflects the content you've put on that particular page. This phrase should be two to four words and should be as specific as possible. When thinking of keyword phrases for a given page, try to imagine what a user would realistically type into a search engine. Once you research how popular a potential keyword phrase is, you may decide to make some adjustments in order to determine the most popular keyword phrases that relate to your content, thus maximumizing the number of hits your site will potentially receive.

Keyword Phrase Research Tools

You can check the popularity and competitiveness of your desired keyword phrase through the following free tools:

Google AdWord Keyword Tool: https://adwords.google.com/select/Keyword ToolExternalWordTracker Keywords: http://freekeywords.wordtracker.com

Sample Keyword Phrase and Title

Let's say that I'm setting up the main page of my business Web site to advertise my new home-based tutoring business (specializing in math instruction) that is located in Houston, Texas. A solid keyword phrase for this page would then be "Houston Math Tutor" because it is descriptive, specific, and performs three times better than "Houston Math Tutoring," according to my quick research. Thus, my page title should look something like this:

Houston Math Tutor—Help Your Child Succeed with a Houston Math Tutor

Notice how I used the keyword phrase twice in the page title. I would also be wise to use the keyword phrase in the page's headline and in the first couple paragraphs of the page's content.

The second step is to make sure that the keyword phrase appears one or two times in the first couple paragraphs of your page's content. This proves to the search-engine algorithm that you have used a keyword phase that is backed up with relevant content on your site. It's also a good idea to use the keyword phrase in the Web page's headline.

As you can see, it isn't complicated or time-consuming to build high-performing keyword phrases into your site's design. Still, effectively utilizing a keyword phrase for each page of your Web site is the easiest and most powerful way to optimize your site for search engines. Of course, there are many other things you can do in this area, but if you focus on keyword phrases when you first set up your site, you'll be off to a strong start.

Google AdWords

An easy and popular way to increase your search-engine visibility is to participate in the Google AdWords program. It only takes a few minutes to set up, and you can use the tool to set up your budget so that the costs will never exceed what you want to spend. The service is results-driven, so you are only charged when a user clicks on your link and ends up at your site. Additionally, you can start, stop, and resume your

Hot Tip

One more search-engine optimization tip: Links are another easy and effective way to boost your search-engine performance. The more you link to other sites (and more importantly, the more they link to you), the higher your search-engine rankings will rise. That's because the search engine's algorithm sees that you are a legitimate source of information and an active part of the larger Web community. Make sure that any links you include on your site add value to the user experience and aren't just gratuitous.

participation in AdWords at any time with just the click of a mouse. Best of all for home-based tutoring businesses, you can set it up so that your link only pops up for local searches. You can designate the search radius on which you want to focus. If online marketing is a large part of your marketing strategy, AdWords is a tool you will definitely want to explore.

Offering Online Support Between Sessions

Outside of business Web sites and marketing tools, you may also be interested in adding an online aspect to your tutoring services. Depending upon the needs and preferences of your students, you may discover that you can add value to the tutoring experience by designing creative ways to interact with and support your students even when you can't meet in person. With proper planning and communication, this could develop into a new revenue stream for your business.

As your relationships develop with long-term tutoring students, you will likely find that your students will naturally come to rely on you for all of their learning-related needs. Even the students who were initially dragged kicking and screaming to your tutoring table will come to trust you and depend on you for support and guidance. This is a good thing!

Editing and Proofreading Student Work Via E-mail

If you are tutoring students in Language Arts or other subjects that require students to submit essays or reports, you may want to develop a routine whereby you can review, edit, and proofread their writings before submission to the classroom teacher. This is an effective way to improve the quality of a student's work, which directly translates into higher grades. In turn, your clients will be increasingly satisfied with your work. It's impossible to ignore the improvement that a qualified adult's proofreading and feedback can offer. Classroom teachers will also notice a concrete increase in the quality of the student's work.

Ideally, tutors should guide their students through the revision process in person and as a team. This type of one-on-one focused work provides the most powerful impact on student learning and progress. The tutor is thus able to explain all applicable strategies and techniques that the student needs to integrate into their writing skills repertoire. Aim to edit written work during regular in-person tutoring sessions, whenever possible.

That said, the situation may arise where a face-to-face meeting is impossible to set up. In such cases, you can arrange for students to e-mail you their written work as e-mail attachments and then offer your feedback electronically.

One of the easiest and clearest ways to facilitate online proofreading support is to use the "Track Changes" function offered in Microsoft Word. When you receive a student's essay via e-mail, open the document in Word and go to Tools, then Track Changes (or hit Control + Shift + E). This turns on a function that tracks and marks any changes that you make to the text, whether it's a deletion or an insertion. Go through the essay and make all of your suggested changes just as you would otherwise. The Track Changes function will make it clear to the next person who reads the document exactly what changes you think should be made. When you're done, hit save and e-mail the saved document back to your student, who can then right-click on each suggested change and either accept or reject the suggestion. Of course, you will want to train your students on this function and make sure that they also use Word for their word-processing work.

One potential pitfall to this process is if your editing and proofreading is done in a vacuum without any explanation to or input from the student. You can imagine that many students would opt to take the easy way out and have you do the hard work of revision for them while they just sit back and watch TV, waiting for your e-mailed response. That's why it's important to build into the essay-editing process a way for you to explain to the student why you suggested the changes you did, what strengths and weaknesses you notice in the student's writing, and what changes you expect to see in future essays. Without this critical piece, your students are going to keep making the same mistakes over and over, and you won't see any improvement with time. Even worse, your students would be receiving higher grades on their written work, without earning the improved grade point average through a corresponding increase in knowledge. That's not the type of lesson we should be teaching our students!

To avoid this problem, consider accompanying each proofread essay with a ten-minute phone conference with the student to review your observations and suggestions. Try to emphasize one particular learning point in your discussion and make sure the student knows that you expect to see this problem disappear in future writings. You may also consider outlining your observations in an e-mail to the student, but you can't be certain that the student is really reading and absorbing your words in this scenario. Instead, they could be simply skipping to the attached document and right-clicking through all of the suggested changes without a single thought as to why you've recommended the revisions.

Another creative solution to this potential problem is to only proofread or edit a certain portion of the essay (for example, half of it). Over the phone or via e-mail, tell the student about the mistakes you've noticed and what kinds of changes need to be made, with a few examples to illustrate what you mean. The student is then responsible for revising the rest of the essay independently. This is a great way to find a happy medium between giving the student all the answers and leaving him or her to sink or swim alone.

Hot Tip

If a student sends me an essay to review and it's obvious he or she hasn't done her own basic level of editing before sending it to me, I immediately send it back and ask the student to proofread the work more thoroughly before asking for my help. I am especially strict with this rule when the student has left many obvious mistakes in the essay, particularly skills and concepts that I've already covered during tutoring sessions. Typos, poor punctuation, not following the teacher's assignment—these are not acceptable errors that I should be fixing for the student. I am not offering my proofreading services so that I can perform the student's core responsibilities. Rather, my aim is to help the student expand his or her writing strategies into new areas with increasing competence.

Answering Student Questions

Another way to help your students improve their performance in school is to be available to them to answer questions and provide guidance in between tutoring sessions. If students only see you once or twice a week, it's inevitable that they will need your help on days when they aren't scheduled to see you. You could serve as an "on-call" resource for topics ranging from where to find reliable information online for research reports to how to solve a particularly tricky math problem—or maybe a student feels stuck on how to begin an essay. With a few minutes of support and expertise, you can turn a student's outlook from confusion to confidence.

Pricing Online Services

It's poor business practice to offer something valuable for free. As educators, we tend to be overly generous with our services out of the goodness of our large hearts and caring natures. But as business owners, it's unwise to sell ourselves short and give clients our time and expertise without expecting fair remuneration.

Preempt any pro bono work by building prices for your online services into your fee structure, communicating this clearly to clients at the initial meeting. They may not be interested in opting for this service at first, but as time goes on, and students start to rely on you more and more (with proven results), clients will likely realize that your online support services could be a valuable way to extend their children's learning beyond regular tutoring sessions.

There are several ways to consider pricing your online work with students:

- *As a proportion of your regular hourly rate.* Let's suppose that you normally charge $60 per hour for tutoring sessions; if you spend ten minutes helping a student via e-mail, then you would charge the client $10 for that service on the next invoice.
- *As a flat rate per use.* For instance, you could decide to charge $10 for every simple e-mail question and $20 for editing a lengthier essay with detailed feedback and proofreading.
- *Built into the hourly rate.* Consider offering two options for hourly tutoring rates. For example, $40 per hour for standard tutoring services with no online support (or optional add-on flat-rate support on an as-needed basis), or $45 per hour, which includes unlimited online support.

Watch Out!

If you're not careful, providing off-hours online tutoring support can become something of a monster. I've had students send me an essay at ten o'clock at night with a panicked message about how they need my feedback within an hour because the essay is due the next morning.

When you begin an online tutoring support relationship with a student, make sure to review the guidelines beforehand so that your expectations are clear to all. Explain that online tutoring support is a privilege, and students should plan ahead in order to be respectful of the tutor's schedule and personal life. A few good rules for you to start with are:

- Allow for at least a twenty-four-hour turnaround.
- All written work must be pre-edited and proofread by the student before being e-mailed for review. If an essay has many obvious mistakes, it will be sent back to the student for further work before you review it.
- If you offer specific suggestions or corrections, you should expect the student to take the feedback to heart and integrate it into his or her work both now and in the future.

Naturally, some clients will be inclined to sign up for an online tutoring component, while others will not be interested. Still, it's a good business strategy to design an array of full-service tutoring options so your clients know they can rely on you for all of their learning needs—any day of the week. This also builds on your business's good reputation, as your extra effort will undoubtedly translate into higher scores for the students, serving to strengthen your image as a reliable and results-oriented expert.

Expanding Your Business into Online Tutoring

An article on Entrepreneur.com proclaimed that online tutoring is a "$115 million market [and] one of the hottest areas, especially for high school and middle school students." But what exactly is online tutoring? And can you make it work as the sole emphasis of your business?

Many online-only tutoring businesses operate as multi-tutor 24/7 portals through which clients can access a qualified tutor for a set hourly rate via a live chat interface. The fanciest online tutoring sites combine instant messaging software with an interactive drawing board so that tutor and student can work together by staying on the same page visually. It may prove challenging for an individual tutor to compile all of the necessary high-tech tools and personnel required to offer an array of always-available expertise. Then there's the additional challenge of attracting enough clients to adequately support and monetize your own independent online tutoring company.

However, if this is a tutoring avenue that interests you, I recommend that you do a lot of research and set a detailed budget to begin working toward your goal. Every big company starts somewhere. If you're up for it, go ahead and dream big, and be prepared to work hard. You may even want to work for a while as an online tutor at an already-established company in order to get a feel for the methodology, and to see what improvements you could make with your own endeavor.

12 Business Endgame

Even with a business as dynamic and challenging as home-based tutoring, it's a good idea to visualize how you want your business to grow and evolve with time. Stagnant businesses lag behind the times, cause client interest to wane, and ultimately bore their owners into passivity. Instead, pledge to create an ever-growing, resilient tutoring business right from the start. All it takes is a little imagination and deliberate steps toward a fulfilling professional future.

Visualizing the Evolution

It may seem odd to envision your business's endgame when perhaps you haven't even signed your first client yet. However, there's no time like the

Reasons to Grow Your Business

There are many reasons why business owners might decide to expand their endeavors in new directions, including:

- Increase revenues
- Pursue new interests
- Learn new skills
- Love of a challenge
- Expand business's impact in the community
- Maintain enthusiasm for the industry

Questions to Ask Yourself

How can I expand my base of potential customers?

Am I open to eventually hiring employees to further my business's growth?

How can I increase the number of available tutoring hours in the day or week?

What areas of instruction capture my interest? Can these topics or strategies be integrated into my tutoring services?

How can I take advantage of opportunities presented through the Internet and other forms of technology?

What new subjects or age ranges am I open to tutoring in the future?

What additional training should I pursue to support my long-term business goals?

present for taking stock of your personal and professional needs and then designing a business that can robustly adapt to any eventual changes.

There are obvious benefits to starting small and simple with your business. As you learn the ropes of being self employed, it may be best to keep your business model simple so that you can focus on the fundamentals. The most important tasks you face as a new home-based tutor are to cultivate a positive reputation in the community and to keep clients satisfied. Thus, it may initially feel overwhelming to try to forecast what your business will look like three to five years down the road.

Still, as you visualize your business's present, take a few minutes to consider possible routes of development for the future. Brainstorm ways that you can attract new clients, apply new strategies, and broaden your horizons in creative directions. Don't be afraid to come up with ideas that might sound impossible or even crazy. Any ideas you come up with now are just that—ideas. You aren't committed irrevocably to any one path or another. Nonetheless, you should write down specific thoughts, because you never know what ideas might sound appealing and "just right" in a few years time.

Ways to Grow Your Business

There are dozens of ways that an individual could decide to grow his or her home-based tutoring business. The only criteria are:

- Does the plan work well with your lifestyle?
- Are you qualified to implement the plan?
- Do you have access to the required capital?
- Is there an available market for your expanded services?

If the answers to these questions are "yes," then by all means, pursue a new direction when the timing is right. As long as you and the other members of your household are enthusiastically on board for a new challenge, why not follow your business's natural evolution down the path toward new adventures?

Expanded Days and Hours

The easiest, and perhaps most obvious, way to grow your business and increase income is by offering additional days and hours of availability to your clients. There's a direct correlation between number of tutoring hours per week and business revenue. So, if you need extra income from your tutoring business, see if you can find extra hours in the day or week. Of course, these newfound hours must match up with the hours that your clients are regularly available. For instance, it doesn't do much good to offer Wednesday-morning hours if your students are typical fourth graders at the local public school. But perhaps you could add a few hours by working with homeschooling students.

Get creative and see if you can come up with solutions you never thought of before that would accommodate additional tutoring hours in your weekly schedule. If you normally begin your tutoring day at 3:30 p.m. when school-aged students are first available, maybe with a little research you'll discover that a nearby school offers a weekly minimum day that would allow you to start at 1:30 p.m. once a week.

Hire Employees or Take on a Partner

Another way to grow your business is to increase its power and reach by bringing on additional people. This may take the form of hiring employees that you then match up with clients, serving as something of a tutoring broker and taking a percentage of the revenue. Or, you might consider taking on a partner to share the responsibilities of running your tutoring business. If your business goals are ambitious and complex, you may only be able to accomplish your objectives by including additional people in your plans and execution.

While delineating the details of hiring employees is beyond the scope of this book, you may want to look into hiring a payroll company to help you comply with the many laws and regulations that come along with new hires. This decision could also imply a need to change the business structure in order to maximize tax benefits and minimize other liabilities. If you decide to hire employees or take on a partner, consult an accountant and/or business attorney for guidance and support.

Tutor a New Age Group

Another easy way to branch out and explore new tutoring avenues is through expanding your services to include new age groups. If you tutor school-aged children, is there a way to apply your expertise to older students? For example, high school English tutors could conceivably apply those skills to college students, whether at community college or university. Or maybe your writing wisdom could help adults write résumés and cover letters during job hunts. Or perhaps you're an SAT tutor who, with a little extra time and effort, could become an expert at other standardized tests, such as the Test of English as a Foreign Language (TOEFL), or even the Graduate Record Examinations (GRE) that students take to get into graduate school.

On the flip side, if you tutor older students or adults, would you be interested in working with younger students? Some tutors are uncomfortable working with younger students, so it's important to be realistic about what kind of work you will enjoy doing.

Simply put, if you're in need of—or simply want to take on—more students, the most direct way is to expand your market of potential clients. If you're unsure, perhaps you should start slowly by taking on only one new client of the new age level and see how it goes. If you feel satisfied and are achieving proven results, it just may be that you've broadened your horizons and increased your business's revenue in one easy step.

Move Online

As discussed in chapter 11, there are various ways to incorporate online tools into your home-based tutoring repertoire. With a little creativity, determination, and hard work, you can develop high-tech plans that you can then implement and monetize from the comfort of your own desk. For example, if you decide to hire employees and serve as a tutoring broker, you can set up a Web site to help you recruit interested tutors to join your venture and to market your expanded services.

The Benefits of Staying Small

Some home-based tutoring business owners may opt to keep their organizations small and simple, rather than expanding in grand ways. While every business will inevitably evolve with time, you may not necessarily want to take your business to a more complex and involved level. Particularly if you hire additional employees or take on a partner, there are certain complicating issues that you should take into account before proceeding down this path. In fact, there are a few key benefits to keeping your business small, tight, and focused. It's up to you to weigh the pros and cons in order to make the right decision for your business.

Flexibility

One of the major perks of being self-employed is the ability to call your own shots. The more intricate your business becomes, the more your personal and professional flexibility will naturally be compromised. For example, if your business functions as a one-person tutoring machine, you can vacation whenever you like, as long as you plan ahead and communicate clearly to your clients. When you start to bring on employees or partners in your business, there will be additional people to consult who will have their own ideas and issues that could complicate any given situation, beyond just vacation times. However, if your business remains small and simple, you can add more clients, change your schedule, or branch into new subject areas with speed and efficiency. When you alone are 100 percent responsible for all business decisions, you can shape your professional life to fit whatever you envision. And isn't that one of the reasons you started this business in the first place?

Hands-On Control

Another great benefit to owning a home-based business is that, as the sole owner, you maintain total control over any and all business decisions that must be made. By keeping your business lean, mean, and firmly in your control, you ensure that your professional life will always reflect your personal core values and intentions. You avoid the risk of watching "your baby" morph into an organization that you no longer recognize as a reflection of your original plans. With no one to ask for permission, you can move the business in whatever direction you decide at any given time—in both the short- and the long term. By maintaining a personal, hands-on approach, you guarantee that you have full awareness of and command over every last detail. You can make sure that every client is satisfied and each student is progressing in the right direction. Just as important, you can address any problems—large or small—quickly and with personal attention.

Focus

A simple business structure allows you to focus on what really matters: helping your students learn and succeed. As the sole owner and tutor, you can zone in with laser precision on your business's objectives and make them come to fruition. Without having to turn your attention to larger or more complex issues, your focus can remain sharp and clear. If you excel at multitasking, perhaps the idea of broadening your attention in various directions sounds appealing. However, if you feel more comfortable doing one or two things very well, perhaps it's best to embrace one of the benefits of staying small—the ability to focus on what was really important to you when you started the company in the first place.

13 Training and Certification

When you work for someone else, ongoing training is often mandatory in order to maintain employment, earn raises, and get promotions. However, when you are self-employed, it can be all too easy to ignore your own professional growth because there's no boss above you waiting to check up on your attendance at seminars. Still, that's no excuse for stagnation. Seeking out relevant training opportunities not only helps your business practices evolve, but it also steers you clear of coming to a personal and professional standstill. Just like your students, you will feel a sense of accomplishment and renewed commitment to your work when you learn and apply new skills that help you reach your goals.

Staying Connected to Educational Trends and Tools

As a rule, classroom teachers find it easy to stay informed on the latest learning trends and tools. Between staff meetings and mandatory training sessions, professional growth is practically inevitable.

Outside of a professional community, private tutors will have to be intrinsically motivated to seek out and create ways to stay in tune with the latest instructional research and its application with students. Ignoring or minimizing your professional development will result in a stagnant approach to learning that your clients will sense and feel an aversion to. Parents are aware of how classroom teachers work with students, so if your methods and/or language differ greatly from that of the larger learning community, you will stand out and your services may not appeal to a broad range of savvy clients.

It may take a little extra work to develop your skills and strategies, but you will reap tangible benefits—both personal and professional—from your efforts. Ongoing training:

- helps you stay current with the latest educational research and new pedagogical strategies;
- enhances your résumé to attract new clients (and maintain current ones)
- offers networking opportunities that can help your business grow and evolve;
- makes home-based tutoring a less solitary experience by giving you the chance to get out into the world and interact with other adults in education; and
- maintains your interest in and enthusiasm for tutoring as a profession.

Ways to Grow Professionally

So how can at-home tutors stay current with the latest pedagogical research and find opportunities to brainstorm with other professionals? Depending on your interests, budget, and business goals, there are various avenues for exploring the latest methodologies in education while expanding your horizons in new ways.

Attend Professional Training Seminars

If you've ever worked as a classroom teacher, you know that each state's Department of Education requires that teachers participate in a minimum number of training hours annually, in order to maintain an active teaching license for employment. Who says that these seminars and training events are open only to classroom teachers? Ask a friendly classroom teacher for referrals to interesting training opportunities. A current classroom teacher will likely know about the latest trends

Don't Forget about the Business Side

Remember that you're not just an educator, but also a business owner, so you should explore seminars that teach small business owners how to increase their effectiveness, power, and reach. In fact, if you are an experienced educator, you may need to focus more on developing your business-owning acumen than on learning about the latest teaching strategies. Or better yet, do a mix of the two topics, perhaps alternating business training one year and teaching courses the next.

and newest teaching techniques that teachers are buzzing about. Many of these techniques will likely be even more effective when used in one-on-one tutoring rather than with larger groups of students. Be aware that these seminars are sometimes costly; but if you build training costs into your budget (and perhaps attend only one carefully chosen training event per year), it may still be something that works for you and your business.

Subscribe to Educational Journals

Regularly reading education publications is a low-cost way to keep your finger on the pulse of the latest developments in teaching and learning. Many educational journals are published online where you can read some of the content from the printed magazine for free. For a subscription fee, you can access 100 percent of the magazine's monthly content. (Remember to keep a receipt for any purchased subscriptions to document the tax write-off.) Alternatively, it might be enough for you to read a few education-related blogs each day. Blogs are almost always free, offering an up-to-the-minute, interactive look at what real teachers are discussing.

Earn Advanced Degrees and/or Specialized Credentials

Formal schooling is a quantifiable and structured way to continue learning about the world of education in practice. If you've already earned your teaching credential, you may want to work toward a specialized certification—for example, in reading instruction—that shows your clients you are an expert in a certain type of teaching. Or, you can take your formal schooling a large step further and earn a master's degree in an education-related discipline. If an accredited program isn't available in

Education Publications

Education Week: www.edweek.org
eSchoolNews: www.eschoolnews.com
International Reading Association Journals (all ages): www.reading.org/General/Publications.aspx
The Mailbox—An Idea Magazine for Teachers: www.theeducationcenter.com
The Teacher: www.teachermagazine.org

your area, look into online options that will allow you to pursue your educational goals on your schedule and from the comfort of your own home.

Participate in Online Teacher Forums

Online teaching communities are an informal way to observe what classroom teachers (and maybe even other private tutors) are discussing and how they are instructing their students. If you step out of lurker mode, you can ask specific questions that relate to your particular situation. I recommend finding a community that is positive and friendly, not just full of complaints and rants. Make sure you practice good online etiquette by contributing your own advice and support to other educators, not just asking for help without giving anything in return. After all, you're an experienced and practicing educator, too!

Read the Latest Books on Teaching Methodology and Theory

Through the latest education books, professional growth can happen in the comfort of your own home and on your own schedule. Talk to other active classroom teachers to see what ideas are spreading like wildfire on their campuses. When I was a classroom teacher, there were always two or three books that everyone was reading and trying out in the classroom. Or, check out an online bookseller's rankings of best-sellers by genre.

Look for practical books full of teaching strategies that are easy to implement and proven to be effective. As a one-on-one tutor, you will benefit most from exploring a variety of usable new techniques so that both you and your students don't get bored with the same old selection of approaches. You can mix up your reading list with inspirational books for teachers that hearten your spirit, as well as educational theory treatises. Consult the appendix of this book for a list of recommended titles.

Hot Tip

Start or join a book club with other home-based educators in your community, or search for relevant online book clubs. Sharing a commitment to professional development with other teachers and tutors will help keep everyone in the club motivated and moving forward.

Network with Educators and Private Tutors in Your Community

Working from home can sometimes feel like a solitary, even lonely, endeavor, especially if you work with young children and rarely interact with other adults. So while it takes a little extra effort to network with other local educators and tutors, it can keep you sane and energized to meet up with other professionals to discuss common issues, brainstorm solutions, or even just to blow off steam together. Just because you work from home doesn't mean you are stuck within your four walls. There's power and support to be found in the hearts and minds of other professionals who are doing the same type of work you are. So take a chance and introduce yourself to your "colleagues." You never know how this simple step might improve both your business prospects and your personal outlook.

Above All, Keep It Practical

Ongoing professional training shouldn't feel like a chore or just another task on your to-do list. That's why, above, all, I recommend that you focus on practical training opportunities that are immediately relevant to your business and/or your students. If you are gaining usable tools and insight that further your business goals and help your students succeed, you will feel energized by seminars that give you the chance to expand your repertoire and open your eyes to new ways to work effectively. And when you consistently build professional training into your annual schedule and budget, you just might find that it's what keeps you interested in education for the long haul.

Tutoring Organizations

The Association for the Tutoring Profession: www.myatp.org
National Tutoring Association: www.ntatutor.com
Tutoring associations specific to your state or region

Appendix

Recommended Reading List

Business

Biafore, Bonnie. *QuickBooks 2009: The Missing Manual.* Sebastopol, CA: O'Reilly Media, 2009.

Covey, Stephen R. *The 7 Habits of Highly Effective People.* New York: Free Press, 2004.

Flannery, David A. *Bookkeeping Made Simple.* New York: Broadway Books, 2005.

Kanarek, Lisa. *Home Office Solutions: Creating a Space that Works for You.* Bloomington, IN: Quarry, 2004.

Walkenbach, John. *Excel 2007 Bible.* Indianapolis, IN: Wiley, 2007.

Warner, Janine C. *Web Sites for Dummies: Do-It-Yourself.* Hoboken, NJ: Wiley, 2008.

Weems, Mandi. *Getting Clients and Keeping Clients for Your Service Business: A 30-Day Step-by-Step Plan for Building Your Business.* Ocala, FL: Atlantic Publishing Company, 2008.

Teaching

Canfield, Jack, and Mark Victor Hansen. *Chicken Soup for the Teacher's Soul: Stories to Open the Hearts and Rekindle the Spirit of Educators.* Deerfield Beach, FL: Health Communications, 2002.

Fried, Robert L. *The Passionate Teacher: A Practical Guide.* Boston: Beacon Press, 2001.

Goudvis, Anne, and Stephanie Harvey. *Strategies that Work: Teaching Comprehension for Understanding and Engagement.* Portland, ME: Stenhouse, 2007.

Miller, Debbie. *Teaching with Intention: Defining Beliefs, Aligning Practice, Taking Action, K–5*. Portland, ME: Stenhouse, 2008.

Silver, Harvey F., Richard W. Strong, and Matthew J. Perini. *So Each May Learn: Integrating Learning Styles and Multiple Intelligences.* Alexandria, VA: Association for Supervision & Curriculum Development, 2000.

Recommended Web Sites

Tutoring Organizations

The Association for the Tutoring Profession: www.myatp.org

National Tutoring Association: www.ntatutor.com

Tutoring associations specific to your state or region

Professional Journals

Education Week: www.edweek.org

eSchoolNews: www.eschoolnews.com

International Reading Association Journals (all ages): www.reading.org/General/Publications.aspx

The Mailbox—An Idea Magazine for Teachers: www.theeducationcenter.com

The Teacher: www.teachermagazine.org

Tax Information

Internal Revenue Service (IRS) Small Business and Self-Employed Tax Center: www.irs.gov/businesses/small

U.S. Small Business Administration Tax Guide: www.sba.gov/smallbusinessplanner/manage/paytaxes

Small Business Resources

Entrepreneur.com: www.entrepreneur.com/bizstartups

Internal Revenue Service: www.irs.gov

Legal Zoom: www.legalzoom.com

Service Corps of Retired Executives (SCORE): www.score.org

Small Business Association (SBA): www.sba.gov

Teaching Tools
(Can also be recommended for students to use independently at home)

Elementary

Free Reading Motivation Program: www.bookadventure.com
Language Arts and Social Studies: www.timeforkids.com
Multiple-Subject Games: www.funbrain.com

Middle and High School

Homework High: www.channel4learning.net/apps/homeworkhigh
Math Tutorials and Games: www.mathgoodies.com
Quizzes, Puzzles, and More: www.highschoolace.com

SAT Preparation

Free Online Prep: www.number2.com
Official SAT Question of the Day: www.collegeboard.com/apps/qotd/question
Vocabulary Development: www.freerice.com

Miscellaneous

Graphic Organizers: www.eduplace.com/graphicorganizer
Multiple Subjects: www.discoveryeducation.com
Reading: www.beyondbooks.com
Writing: www.webenglishteacher.com

Web-Site Building Tools

Google AdWord Keyword Tool: https://adwords.google.com/select/KeywordTool
ExternalWeebly (free Web design and hosting): www.weebly.com
WordTracker Keywords: http://freekeywords.wordtracker.com

Recommended Software and Sources

Word-Processing and Spreadsheet

GoogleApps: www.google.com/apps
Microsoft Office (Word and Excel): http://office.microsoft.com
OpenOffice: www.openoffice.org

Accounting-Specific (all available in free versions at http://download.com)

BillQuick Lite

Intuit QuickBooks

Microsoft Office Accounting Express

Frequently Asked Questions (FAQs)

I feel overwhelmed by everything I have to do to start my own tutoring business. What should be my first step?

Besides assessing your personal and professional strengths, it's best to start by performing in-depth market research to make sure that you will be able to find enough clients to support your business goals. You can write the best business plan and set up the most polished Web site, but it won't do any good if there isn't a viable market for your skills and services. Knowledge of your surrounding market will help you streamline your efforts as you set up the business and help you tailor your services to what the community really needs. After the market research is complete, you can move on to more concrete steps, such as setting up your home office and filing for your business name and/or license.

What is your favorite part about being a home-based tutor?

On a surface level, I appreciate the flexibility that comes along with working from home and setting my own schedule. But what I really enjoy is forming one-on-one relationships with my students. I love getting to know my students' unique personalities, how their brains work, and how I can best apply my skills to meet their educational needs.

What is the most challenging part of starting a home-based tutoring business?

Depending on each business owner's individual strengths and weaknesses, the challenges can vary. For many former classroom teachers, it might initially feel foreign to start thinking like a business owner. Tasks like filing for a business name and forecasting a multifaceted annual budget could feel especially challenging at first. But with proper planning, hard work, and a little practice, these business-related tasks will quickly become as easy to perform as presenting an effective lesson plan to a student. None of the tasks associated with starting a home-based tutoring business is particularly overwhelming on its own. Don't focus on what appears challenging; instead, arm yourself with information and dive in with enthusiasm.

How much can I expect to charge hourly for my tutoring services?

This varies greatly by region, subject areas, student age, and the specific market in your community, as well as your level of expertise. At the lower end of the range, a noncertified, beginning college student tutor might be able to charge a minimum of $20 per hour, whereas a tutor with a master's degree in math could charge up to $100 per hour for sharing his or her expertise with older students.

How many hours per week are required to own a home-based tutoring business?

Again, this varies greatly depending upon how much you want to work, how available your prospective clients are on a daily and weekly basis, and how successful you are at marketing your business and securing clients. A tutor's workload could potentially range from five to thirty-plus hours per week with students, plus five to ten hours of "back office" work for accounting, invoicing, planning lessons, communicating with clients, and performing other business maintenance routines.

What are the estimated start-up costs for a home-based tutoring business?

If you are willing to do much of the preliminary legwork and research on your own, it could cost as little as $500 to set up your company from scratch, especially if you are creative with sourcing used teaching materials and are careful to buy only the minimum required tools to start. If, however, you hire experts (such as an accountant and/or business attorney) to support your objectives, the start-up costs could range from $1,000 to $2,000, or maybe more. It's up to you how much of the initial work you want to do on your own. Hiring an expert who offers guidance will likely save you time, but it comes at a price. Besides, doing the work yourself offers a chance to gain valuable in-depth knowledge of how your business is structured from the ground up.

Is a business Web site a required component of a home-based tutoring business?

With a home-based tutoring business, it's definitely not required to have an online presence. However, it's so easy and inexpensive to create a Web site with today's tools that the small time investment might make it a worthwhile option to explore. When you have a simple Web site to represent your business, you offer potential clients a convenient way to learn about your services and get your contact information.

Can I write off my home office on my tax return?

The Internal Revenue Service (IRS) is strict about who they allow to write off portions of a home for tax purposes. If you use an area of your home exclusively for business and the area serves as the primary place where you meet with clients and run the business, then speak to an accountant about whether you can write off your home office or not. It's best not to seek this write-off unless you are certain it applies, because home office write-offs are a major red flag to IRS auditors.

Is it mandatory to consult with a business attorney before starting my business? How can I protect myself from clients who don't pay their bills?

Consider obtaining prepaid legal insurance. For as little as $1 a day, you have access to attorneys who specialize in your type of business. The insurance entitles you to be able to ask an attorney questions to clarify how you should proceed. Additionally, legal services will be available to you in case of delinquent payments, problems with competitors, or any other potential liabilities that come along with owning your own business.

How can I build buzz in the community about my business? How can I make my services stand out from those of other tutors?

The most direct path to positive business buzz is to give your students a pleasant and productive experience at each and every tutoring session. Communicate clearly and proactively with your clients on a regular basis. Plan quality customized lessons that meet each student's assessed needs and that work toward specific learning goals. When your focused work starts to yield quantifiable and undeniable results, your clients will be thrilled with their choice to hire you. Best of all, they will share their enthusiastic satisfaction with other potential clients who might be interested in your services, too.

Index

About the Author

Beth A. Lewis has worked in the education field for ten years, as both a classroom teacher and as a home-based tutor. She has taught third grade in an award-winning Title I elementary school as well as high school English, journalism, and SAT preparation at a private institution. Beth now tutors students in a wide range of subjects and grade levels, including second graders who need help with reading all the way up to high school seniors preparing for the SAT. Through her work as the About.com Guide to Elementary Education for the past ten years and counting, Beth supports educators around the world by offering effective classroom-ready solutions through her blog and collection of practical articles. Beth lives in San Diego, California with her husband Daniel.